THE CRY OF MUTE CHILDREN

'Ilany Kogan has written a powerful and astute book on the psychoanalytic treatment of the offspring of Holocaust survivors, drawing on her experience of being an analyst to some of their sons and daughters. Through an in-depth, sensitive presentation of eight analyses conducted with children of survivors, the author shows how the shadow of the Holocaust sets the state for the intrapsychic drama played out by the second generation during the course of their analytic journey. These patients grapple with the meaning of the Holocaust – conscious and unconscious – in their own lives as well as the lives of their parents.

Ilany Kogan's style is unique. She provides a depth and richness of detail in her patients' fantasy worlds, as well as her own experience of countertransference. She invites the reader to participate in the vicissitudes of the analytic process, including moments of frustration, analytic impasses and ruptures in the therapeutic alliance. Through her open, unassuming style, her well-organized writing and the judicious use of verbatim material, the author breathes life into these analytic stories.

The important insights revealed in this book can inform us not only in the realm of this particular group of patients but all those whose lives are touched by the reality of war, violence and trauma.'

Dr Ann Adelman
Yale University

'Ilany Kogan's vivid description of the psychological fate of children of the survivors of Auschwitz and other Nazi death camps alerts us to the long-lasting effects of severe trauma and its transmission from one generation to the next. Dehumanisation is a constant feature of human history, and this book reminds us of our need to be vigilant in the defence of civilisation.'

Dr Dinora Pines
London

'Ilany Kogan has written a book with so many truths in it that it should be required reading for all those colleagues who might be consulted by members of the second generation.'

Professor Martin Wangh
Jerusalem

The author: Ilany Kogan is a psychoanalyst and clinical psychologist, living and working in Israel. She is also a teacher and supervisor at the Department of Psychotherapy in the Medical School of Tel-Aviv University. She has presented numerous papers on her work at conferences throughout Europe, North America and in Israel, and is a member of the Steering Committee of the International Trauma Centre, Yale University.

THE CRY OF MUTE CHILDREN

A psychoanalytic perspective of the second generation of the Holocaust

Ilany Kogan

FREE ASSOCIATION BOOKS / LONDON / NEW YORK

Published in 1995 by
Free Association Books Ltd
Omnibus Business Centre
39–41 North Road
London N7 9DP

95 96 97 98 99 5 4 3 2 1

ISBN 1 85343 321 7 – hbk
ISBN 1 85343 322 5 – pbk

A CIP catalogue record for this book is available
from the British Library.

Produced for Free Association Books Ltd by
Chase Production Services, Chipping Norton.
Typeset by Stanford Desktop Publishing, Milton Keynes.
Printed in the EC by T J Press, Padstow, England.

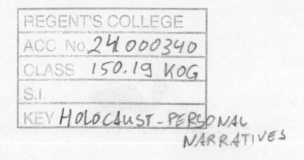

Contents

This book is dedicated to the memory of
Prof. Hillel Klein, teacher and friend.

'I was once more struck by the truth of the ancient saying: Man's heart is a ditch full of blood. The loved ones who have died throw themselves down on the bank of this ditch to drink the blood and so come to life again; the dearer they are to you, the more of your blood they drink.'

Nikos Kazantzakis, Zorba the Greek

Acknowledgements

I would like to thank some of my teachers and friends around the world who helped me in various ways over the past years.

Dr. Yolanda Gampel, who shared with me her knowledge and understanding of working with the second generation, and opened up new fields of vision for me, for which I am greatly indebted.

Dr. Dinora Pines, with whom a long-standing friendship has been built on our common interest in the analysis of Holocaust survivors and their offspring, and who has been a constant source of encouragement.

Prof. Martin Wangh, who has been a supportive friend and teacher.

Dr. Dori Laub, whose love and friendship for Hillel Klein brought us together and made us partners in various scientific projects.

Mme Janine Chasseguet-Smirgel for her loyalty to the Israeli audience, and for being an active participant in various psycho-analytic conferences which I had the honour of organising in Israel. I would like to point out her courageous approach to the topic of Nazi Germany and the Holocaust, as well as her involvement in the study of it.

Dr. Judith Kestenberg, my honoured friend, for reading and commenting on some of my papers.

Mrs. Anne-Marie Sandler, for her critical review of my work, from which I learned much.

Dr. Joseph Berke for his friendship and help with the publishing of this book.

Dr. Milton Jucovy for his appreciation and support.

My German colleagues, Dr. Gemma Jappe and Dr. Carl Nedelmann – close friends of Hillel Klein – who became my personal friends as well, and Mr. Herman Beland, Dr. Peter Wegner, Prof. Hans Henseler, Prof. Dieter Ohlmaeir, Mrs. Sibylle Drews,

Dr. Christian Schneider, Mrs. Cordelia Stillke and Dr. Bernward Leineweber for their friendship and appreciation of my work.

I would also like to thank Mr. David Tuckett, editor of the *International Journal of Psychoanalysis*, for his unceasing support. This journal, which published my work when I was a totally unknown young analyst from Israel, has, over the years, given me the wonderful opportunity of acquainting many people around the world with my work.

I want to thank Mrs. Hava Kasel, my English editor, for her dedication and constant assistance, and Mrs. Michelle Simpson for her invaluable and accurate wordprocessing.

Finally, I am grateful to my patients who allowed me to accompany them on their analytic journey.

Preface

My interest over the last ten years in the analytic study of the sons
and daughters of Holocaust survivors is the outcome of my work
and friendship with the late Prof. Hillel Klein, who dedicated his
life to the study of the Holocaust.

My association with Klein began towards the end of my training
at The Israel Psychoanalytic Institute. I began my acquaintance
with him as a student, but I quickly became a friend who helped
him through the last and most difficult period of his life, since
he had been in a concentration camp. During this period Klein
developed cancer of the brain. An operation enabled him to live
another two years and continue his work.

It was during this period that Klein asked me to help him write,
and I became his co-author. Because he was facing death, the
trauma of the Holocaust, his persecution and the painful losses
he had incurred during that time were revivified in his mind. Klein
shared his own shattering experiences with me, as well as his
affective understanding of survivors and their children.

In my opinion, Klein was a gifted, astute, clinical observer
who, with unusual perspicacity, was capable of baring and identifying some of the truths which make up people's psyches. His
own traumatic experiences and losses led him to explore the
extent to which survivors were impaired in their ability to trust
others, to experience intimacy and love, to feel empathy for their
loved ones and to retain the most sensitive qualities of a human
being. At the same time, he felt deeply for survivors, with whom
he identified. An example of this was his fight to 'purge' survivors
of the negative meaning associated with the term 'survivor's
guilt' and turn it into something positive. Klein (1984) felt that
'survivor's guilt' served an adaptive purpose when it linked
survivor and offspring to the past, to those who died, and to a
sense of belonging to the Jewish world.

During the last two years of his life, Klein and I co-authored two articles. The first one was 'Some observations on denial and avoidance in Jewish Holocaust and post-Holocaust experience'. Though very ill, Klein was still able to deliver this paper at the Conference on Denial which took place in Jerusalem in January 1985. The second, 'Identification and denial in the shadow of Nazism', was to be presented at the Congress of the International Psychoanalytic Association in Hamburg, in the plenary lectures dealing with the phenomenon of Nazism. This congress was a very emotionally-laden event for all of us from Israel, as it was the first analytic congress held in Germany since the Second World War. Presenting a paper in Germany at this stage of his life held a special meaning for Klein. He never forgot how he had emerged from the concentration camp a physically- and emotionally-damaged human being.

Klein was tormented throughout his life by his longing for his loved ones who had perished. For many years he refused to visit Germany or speak its language. It was only towards the end of his life that he changed his attitude and agreed to accept the frequent invitations to lecture and supervise there. He was greatly admired in Germany for his talent as an analyst and teacher and was loved for what he was – a survivor.

Klein often talked about his love–hate relationship with Germany and he undoubtedly loved the young German analysts as much as he did his pupils in Israel. Appearing in front of them as a gifted, eloquent analyst, his words, as well as the number tattooed on his arm, never let them forget the past. At the same time, he was exquisitely sensitive to their pain and guilt. Paradoxically, he freed them from an overwhelming sense of guilt by making them responsible in a very personal way for what they were – the sons and daughters of those who had killed his family and persecuted him. In my subsequent visits to Germany, I had the opportunity to learn the extent to which the German analysts considered him a spiritual father. The love and admiration they bestowed upon him was part of his 'vengeance'.

Unfortunately, two months before the Hamburg Congress, Klein became paralysed. Unable to deliver the lecture which would have been the high point of his career, he asked me, as his co-author, to deliver our joint paper. I would like to take this opportunity to express thanks to Mme Chasseguet-Smirgel, the chairperson of the Scientific Committee of the Congress, who also insisted that I deliver the paper. I would also like to thank Prof.

M. Wangh, a close, loyal friend of Klein's, who helped and encouraged me, then only a candidate at the Israel Psychoanalytic Institute, to appear in front of an audience of 3000 people. Wangh's message was very clear: 'You are the second generation – now it is your turn.' Thus, at Klein's death bed, and together with other students who had worked with him at the hospital and in different clinics, I was given the 'message of continuation'. This was conveyed to the German audience in a manner beyond words. It was as if the German analysts mourned Hillel Klein, the survivor, with me, and expected the 'second generation' to take his place.

On my return to Israel I still had the opportunity to tell Klein about the success of our paper, which had been very warmly received by the Congress. He was very sick and was suffering terribly. It was so typical of Klein to fight until his last breath, in spite of his conflictive death wishes (of which he was long aware).

About six months before his death, Klein read the first chapter of this book, 'A Journey Through the Ice Castle', from which the clinical illustration for the Hamburg paper was taken. After reading it, he smilingly called me to his bedside (to which he was confined), and said 'Look what we have here. A writer!', and then, on a more serious note, he suggested that I consider the idea of writing a book. During the last years of his life, Klein had gathered material for a book which, unfortunately, he knew he would never complete. As a true survivor-father, he handed me the legacy of writing this book.

It took time for me to work through the powerful emotional experiences of those last two years. I had accompanied a beloved teacher and friend to his death, and was with him until almost the very end. His family considered me a friend and deeply appreciated the support I had given him during that difficult time. Working through my mourning, I often felt what children of survivors feel – a firm bond to the past as well as a wish to break away from it.

I was aware that I was becoming much closer to my second-generation patients and much more sensitive to their plight. I felt that my analytic task was to help them work through the burden of the past which had been transmitted to them in ways which were beyond words. The creative act of writing, though painful and difficult, helped me work through the mourning, as well as affirm life.

Foreword

Janine Chasseguet-Smirgel

It is now fifty years since the concentration camps were liberated, and this is being commemorated as I write. 'Fifty years on, and we are still remembering and talking about it?' some sigh impatiently. And the strange thing is that the invective of the extreme right, which in my country comes from Le Pen and his friends, is now close to the ideas of some Israelis. There is a current Israeli ideology, rationalised as the need to usher in a new era of post peace-treaty politics (even though the ideology existed long before the peace talks), which uses the mass media to marginalise the significance of the Shoah.

After screenings of Claude Lanzmann's film, the University of Bar-Ilan organised a conference in his honour. One young man, now in an important position at the Hebrew University of Jerusalem, claimed that it is 'obscene' to separate the Shoah from other genocides that have taken place in history.

A few years ago I visited Claude Domenach, then the French cultural attaché in Tel Aviv, and during conversation he asked, indignantly: 'Can you believe all the fuss they make about what happened to them? Have you seen Yad Vashem?' At the time I put it down to his virulent anti-Semitism, carefully concealed from Israel's francophone community (over 20 per cent of the population) who thought of Domenach as a friend. And yet this is, more or less, what Israelis themselves are now saying.

'Beware museums', says a character in *Hametz*, the recent play by Hasfari, a critique of 'Jewish paranoia' (reviewed by Rachel Israel, a psychoanalyst in Tel Aviv, writing for the French magazine *Information Juive*). There is another play which was filmed recently – *Do not touch my Shoah* (Israeli version), or *Bolagen* (German version) – which conveys a similar message. The play's leading actress was interviewed on the Franco-German television channel,

ARTF. This young woman, whose father is a camp survivor, told us how sexually exciting she finds the Nazi song 'Horst Wessel Lied', and how it sounds like Israeli songs and marches (which of course is not true of its lyrics, nor of the music as Israeli songs are directly influenced by Russian and Yiddish music). The daughter of a survivor, she was making the equation: Israelis = Nazis. She says: 'Fuck the six million dead.' The play is acted by Israelis and an Arab, which could be wonderful if it were not for the fact that it depicts a concentration camp where deportees are naked and bound, upside down, in a spine-chilling atmosphere of nauseating eroticism. Whatever the play was about, the actress quoted above was recounting on screen how she had been anorexic during her adolescence and how she used to hide food in her vagina.

Ilany Kogan (an Israeli analyst who has given lectures all over the Western world) tells us of how she hears a different, mute, scream from the children she meets. However painful it seems, we want to take it to heart, as she is able to do. With extraordinary patience she teaches us to find the shards of parents' histories, through their verbal material, but even more often in acts, in entire episodes of the lives of her patients.

The child has often been used, unconsciously, by the parents as a 'container' for their fragmented selves and their pain. Thus their perception of the present is deformed by the vestiges of a past which is not theirs, but which has been imposed upon them. Their behaviour obeys a compulsion of which they are unaware, leading them to kill a kitten by leaving it in an overheated room, to create an accident in which their child dies, to wound a father who has come to rescue them from suicide ... Sometimes it is external reality which seems to be blistering with sinister meaning and unbelievable coincidences which seem to ape the patient's unconscious. It is thus for Rachel, whose young lover dies suddenly in her arms. The unconscious of these patients, having been invaded, occupied and inhabited, begins in turn to kill, wound and mutilate; but is most often turned against the subject themselves. Relationships are dislocated, love is impossible, happiness is forbidden. The shadow of the forests of Poland fall upon the sons and daughters of the survivors. The barbed wire fences can still electrocute, a familiar bedroom becomes a gas chamber ...

The tales of the cases are punctuated by signs and symbols: a dead squirrel, the carcass of a pregnant cat, the smell of rotting, an ice castle, a glass of milk with ashes in it ...

A glass of milk with ashes in it ...

Ilany Kogan's work with her analysands is a sensitive, patient, painful elaboration. The analyst often suffers what the patients cannot bring themselves to experience for themselves, but which they either 'enact' endlessly or project onto the analyst in order to be rid of it. Giving back to her patients in a more coherent form the parts of themselves that were full of the fragments of their parents' histories, of which they too had been invaded, Ilany Kogan enables her patients to be nourished by milk which is no longer poisoned by ashes. The dead can be mourned without reliving their agonies. The self which had previously been absorbed by the parents now finds autonomy. Mortal repetition can given way to life.

So, to those who shout 'Beware museums', the silent cry of these children replies: 'We are the museums in which our parents and our grandparents have locked away their memories, experiences and nightmares. Like them, we die a thousand deaths; as for them, 'Es brennt, briderlich, es brennt'. Like them, we cannot see 'sun shining through the smoke'.

But those who say 'Beware museums', or 'Fuck the six million dead', are also trapped in a pitiless battle against the power of their parents' histories and the history of our century. This battle, which results in self-destructive ideology, is a manifestation of the lowest, least elaborated level of regression. Ilany Kogan's patients, however disturbed, are not repeatedly killing the ghosts of the past, since the ghosts are not only experienced as persecutors but also as painfully loved people. These patients have come to ask for help in order to appease their ghosts and to give them tombs. To each his destiny.

If you let yourself become engrossed in this book, the stories of Gabrielle, Rachel, Kay, Josepha, Isaac and Sara will assail you, leaving deep scratches which will turn into long-lasting scars. But by the time you have finished reading, you will have found consolation and comfort in the milk of human kindness.

Translation © Claire Pajaczkowska 1995

Introduction

As time passed, and the Holocaust became distant history to all but a few individuals and families, a new generation of children born to survivor families grew up. Yet little or nothing appeared in the psychiatric or psychoanalytic literature about the terrible effects of the Holocaust on this second generation, even though many of the children of the survivors developed into sophisticated, well-educated adults and had access to sources of treatment. Perhaps, like their parents, they were wary of psychological treatment or, when they did engage in it, the Holocaust was not recognised by either patient or therapist as responsible for the patient's emotional problems (Jucovy, 1992).

Some of the first reports about the second generation emerged from the professional experiences of Sigal (1971, 1973), Rakoff (1966, 1969) and Trossman (1968), who treated children and adolescents born to survivor families. Their studies indicated that the offspring of survivors were particularly at risk for developing emotional problems, although it is certainly true that not all survivors' families had children who were psychologically impaired.

Further contributions dealing with the psychoanalyses of children of survivors appear in a volume edited by Anthony and Koupernik (1973). I will briefly describe some of these cases, as they are rare in the literature of that period.

Laufer (1973) reported the analysis of an adolescent boy whose father died in a concentration camp before the boy was born. The mother and son emigrated to England, where she remarried when the boy was four years old, and died when he was an adolescent. According to Laufer, the analytic material indicated that children of survivors might be particularly vulnerable in certain areas. For example, the boy's fantasies that his mother might have been a prostitute during the Holocaust and that he was illegitimate are characteristic of children of survivors.

1

Furman (1973) described his analytic work with a four-year-old boy who was utterly lacking in mastery of speech, the ability to eat independently and the capacity for self-differentiation. The treatment process was augmented by the therapist's helpful education of the patient's mother, and included suggestions about the importance of providing age-appropriate information about the Holocaust to her son.

A paper by Brody (1973) describing the analysis of the son of a survivor indicated the connection between the father's flight from Nazi persecution and his son's conflicts during adolescence.

Further progress in research on the effects of the Holocaust on members of the second generation was made through Kestenberg's (1972) analytic work with a survivor's son who behaved in a bizarre fashion and treated his analyst as a hostile persecutor.

Finally, in 1982 an entire book, entitled *Generations of the Holocaust*, appeared, edited by Bergmann and Jucovy. This book, which contained psychotherapies, analyses and research, enriched the theoretical as well as the clinical realm of the treatment of survivors and their children through the contributions of Jucovy, Bergmann, Kestenberg, Gampel, Oliver, Herzog and others.

Over the last ten years, research on the second generation has expanded through the work of Auerhahn and Prelinger (1983), Grubrich-Simitis (1984), Laub and Auerhahn (1984), Jucovy (1992). Research about the first generation has been advanced through the work of Wangh (1968a, 1968b and Felman and Laub (1992), and research about those who have not been directly affected by the Holocaust has been documented by Moses (1993a).

The contribution of the present book to the existing literature is the provision of a detailed description of the analyses of offspring of Holocaust survivors and the recurrent problems and conflicts in their lives. It is unique in that it is the only book that focuses exclusively on the psychoanalytical aspects of the work with these sons and daughters. It offers a detailed description of material taken from eight analyses, often illustrated with verbatim exchanges from the sessions. The reader is thus invited to be 'present' at the sessions and can follow the intimate patient–therapist dialogue from a very close perspective.

On an intellectual level, the reader can observe the recurrent themes and conflicts in the lives of children of survivors as well as the problems encountered by the analyst in their treatment. On an emotional level, the reader becomes involved in the story of the treatment as well as the story of the patient, as they unfold before the eyes in the analysis. In this way, the reader becomes acquainted with the patient as well as with the analyst on a deeply humane level.

Here is a brief description of the chapters in this book:

Chapter I explores the transmission of trauma from parent to child up to the third generation. In each generation we see the mother projecting feelings of depression and guilt upon her daughter, who, by identifying with them, is incapable of achieving self-differentiation.

Chapter II presents an illustration of the victory of life over death through the description of an analysis of a Holocaust survivor's daughter. During the analysis, the patient has a dramatic encounter with death when her lover dies in her arms during the act of love, evoking the resurgence of feelings of mourning and guilt which threaten her existence.

Chapter III presents an analysis of a young woman as a developmental process in which the self becomes better integrated. The growth of the self can be seen in analysis through the development of the patient's mode of communication, from the non-verbal communication of an infant to a more advanced mode of communication of a child and finally to a form of adult verbalisation.

Chapter IV explores the restoration of the capacity to feel pain and guilt, illustrated by material from an analysis of a woman whose four-month-old baby died in a car accident due to her reckless driving.

Chapter V presents an illustration of the behavioural phenomenon of concretisation with material taken from the first stages of analysis of a young man who shot and wounded his survivor father during the latter's attempt to save him from suicide.

Chapter VI explores the difficulties in the development of the capacity to fall (and remain) in love in the case of a second-generation patient whose mother lived through the Holocaust as a child.

Chapter VII presents an attempt to find a more appropriate therapeutic approach to children of Holocaust survivors in a situation of existential threat when the analyst finds himself in the same boat as his patient. Chapter VII differs from the other chapters in this book in which second-generation patients encounter personal traumas in their own lives: it deals with the traumatic encounter of the second-generation patients as well as of the

Jewish population of Israel as a whole with a life-threatening
situation.
The Epilogue explores two main themes typical of the case studies
described in the book. The first is the interplay between fantasy
and reality in the lives of second-generation patients; the second
is the struggle to construct a new, separate and more cohesive self
by means of the therapeutic relationship.

This book is based on my clinical experience, through which I
became aware of the anachronistic hold that the parents' past had
upon the child's present. This was expressed especially in the child's
frequent continuation of the parents' feelings of living under a
death sentence, so that the child could not allow himself, whether
through fear or loyalty, to live otherwise. The way in which the
events in the parents' lives were lived out often demonstrated that
not only the content but also the style of trauma was re-enacted.
These children's character structure, defensive and adaptive styles
as well as life choices often showed the disintegrative effect of a
traumatic event that could not be adequately known, understood
and remembered. The trauma was retained as a discordant, encap-
sulated event, out of reach of reason, insight or reflection. It had
the power to eclipse life or induce a break in life's procession via
solitary re-enactments or permeation of life as a whole. Such
transmission interfered with generalised adaptive functions such
as comprehending, feeling, relating and especially taking charge
of one's life and destiny (Peskin *et al.*, 1995).

Other research has suggested that children of survivors are
likely to experience fear and mistrust in the world (Freyberg,
1980; Fogelman, 1988; Shoshan, 1989), to have problems in the
area of affect regulation and affect tolerance (Adelman, 1993;
Wilson, 1985), and to experience depression and a prolonged sense
of mourning (Shoshan, 1989; Fresco, 1984; Freyberg, 1989). Some
authors have explored issues relating to the psychoanalytic
treatment of children of survivors. Wilson (1985) writes that
children of survivors in therapy can acquire greater affect tolerance
through the joint construction, with the analyst, of 'a historical
narrative which includes the Holocaust legacy'.

The construction of an unbroken narrative – one that fills in
the gaps of the child's knowledge, that permits the saying of
what has been unsayable, that interweaves the knowledge of the
past and present with the realities and the horrors of the Holocaust
– permits the child of survivors to gradually gain some sense of

comfort with what had been split-off and unacknowledged affects and fears. This conceptualisation of the therapeutic framework for the psychoanalytic treatment of children of Holocaust survivors is reflected in this book, mainly in the advanced phase of treatment, the working-through phase, which is a joint endeavour of the patient and the analyst.

Through this phase, I became impressed with the internal psychic change which occurred when therapeutic intervention brought new awareness and enabled the working-through of Holocaust re-enactments between parents and child. As a result of this, the hidden resources of the offspring were often activated in the therapeutic encounter, as shown in the different chapters.

In order to counter the overwhelming presence of death which was often expressed in these cases, I had to be perceived by the patients throughout therapy as actively cathecting life, even after an experience which represented the negation of life. Sometimes, in order to counter the negative outcome brought about by the repetition compulsion, I had to propose actively the possibility of a different outcome. Often it was only by deep belief in a new outcome and in the non-absoluteness of the destruction wrought by the Holocaust that these children could allow themselves to believe that such a possibility could even exist. My recognition of a life-force hidden even in the death imprint of a second trau- matisation (a traumatisation which happened in the patients' present life), or even revelatory from behind it, made me intervene often in a way that turned the trace of death into an attempt to affirm life. It was my commitment to life – the caring about life and giving birth to it – that characterised my work with these patients as well as the entire tenor of these analyses.

I would like to add here a brief comment about the relevance of my treatment to traumatised patients in general.

In the final chapter of this book I deal with the fate of psycho- analytic treatment during a crisis of existential proportions – the Gulf War. I suggest that during times of global crisis the massive insecurity and regressive pull, which may take hold of patients, might best be met initially with the analyst's reaffirmation of the reality of her presence in the context of an empathic therapeu- tic tie, as opposed to further regression via the interpretation of defences. I believe that this insight, as well as the active cathexis of life, is important not only in the realm of this particular group of patients but also with those whose lives have been touched by the reality of war, violence and trauma.

1 A Journey Through the Ice Castle[1]

'... the fathers have eaten sour grapes and the children's teeth are set on edge'.

Jeremiah ch.31 v.29

This chapter explores the transmission of trauma from parent to child up to the third generation through the analysis of an adult daughter of a Holocaust survivor. Only after many years of analysis was it possible to unravel the different layers of the daughter's personality, beneath which lay the trauma transmitted to the child by the survivor mother. The first phases of analysis dealt with an investigation of the daughter's defences and underlying wishes without connecting them intrinsically to the Holocaust. Only after we managed to work through this manifest level and achieve a 'therapeutic regression aiming at the rebirth of the true self' (Winnicott, 1958), did we succeed in uncovering the layers that included the patient's attitudes and fantasies about the Holocaust.

Case Illustration

Gabrielle, an attractive, thirty-five-year-old woman, sought professional help because of her inability to find fulfilment and happiness in her life and personal relationships. She had been married for twelve years, had two daughters (then aged twelve and eight), and worked as a technician in a medical laboratory. Her marriage was on the verge of collapse and she had the burden of raising a disturbed child. (Her younger daughter was diagnosed at the age of two-and-a-half as having emotional problems.)

Gabrielle was born in 1946, somewhere near the Polish-German border, to a survivor mother and a handicapped father (who had had a glass eye since youth). The family spent three years wandering through Poland before immigrating to Israel, where they lived under very difficult conditions for the first few years. Poor and uneducated, both parents struggled to earn a living. Their marriage was unharmonious and devoid of support and friendship.

Gabrielle's mother was the only surviving member of a large family of brothers and sisters (Gabrielle never knew how many) who had perished, along with their parents, during the Holocaust. Her mother, who was then only seventeen, managed to flee through the forest and save her own life. She emerged from the forest after the war limping, emaciated and suffering from rheumatic fever, which developed into a heart condition after Gabrielle's birth. At the age of forty-five, unable to bear her impaired, restricted life, the mother chose to undergo open-heart surgery and died on the operating table. Ten days later, at the age of twenty-three, Gabrielle gave birth to her first daughter, whom she named after her mother.

Gabrielle met her husband during her army service. He was handsome and popular with women. She was very flattered by his interest in her, although she didn't really believe in long-term relationships. She planned to leave him and study medicine, specialising in pathology. However, she became pregnant by him, abandoned her dreams of a career and married him.

Gabrielle's daughter was born several months after her marriage. She was a pleasant, quiet baby who developed normally. Three years later, she and her husband decided to have another child. This baby seemed different from their firstborn. She cried incessantly, did not smile at people, rejected the mother, and at two-and-a-half years old was diagnosed as suffering from emotional and developmental problems.

In the meantime, Gabrielle's husband had been accepted to a foreign students' exchange programme. The family moved to Europe where they spent the next six years. During this period, the couple decided on an 'open marriage' arrangement, with each of them searching for relationships outside the marriage. The younger child, as well as the couple, was in therapy while abroad. The little girl underwent play therapy; Gabrielle attended mother–child experimental groups three times a week and the couple went for counselling for their problems.

When she came for treatment, Gabrielle was living apart from her husband. She described their relationship as perverse and sado-masochistic, with painful and humiliating episodes. The husband, who lived and worked in the same city, provided for the girls finan-cially, but otherwise was totally absent from Gabrielle's life as well as from that of his daughters. The continuous suffering associated with raising her disturbed child alone, the imminent collapse of her marriage, and her previous exposure to therapy abroad led Gabrielle to seek help.

Phase I – The manifest level

During this first period, I saw Gabrielle twice a week in psycho-analytically-oriented psychotherapy. Our goal during this phase was to overcome her fear of the therapeutic relationship by working through her main resistances to therapy: (a) her unin-hibited evacuation of anal material; (b) her overt oedipal wishes; and (c) her erotisation of the transference.

(a)   During the first sessions, Gabrielle related a dream which served as a vehicle for expressing her expectations of me and of therapy. In her dream she took her younger daughter to her father's childhood home. She was walking in front of the child without paying attention to her when she suddenly disappeared: the girl had fallen into a sewer and started to drown.

Gabrielle wanted to call the police to save the child, but finally managed to pull her out by her head. In her associa-tions, Gabrielle talked about her recurrent dreams revolving around sewers and toilets. In her dreams she goes to the toilet to empty her bowels; the surroundings are filthy, and people are looking at her from everywhere. She linked the sewer to her vagina, which she perceived as ugly and defective, especially after having borne children.

It seemed to me that Gabrielle was stripping in front of me, showing me her vagina. She was defecating in my presence and was asking me to be an observer, like a child who shows her mother everything in order to obtain con-firmation of the security and appreciation that she needs.

In addition, I felt that Gabrielle was asking me to save her by taking her out of the sewer in which she might drown. Her demand to be saved was vital, and if I were incapable of taking her out 'by the head' – by means of therapy – thus enabling her to be reborn, she would be sentenced for life.

(b) Gabrielle's oedipal wishes, which were connected to anal material, were brought up in therapy on a manifest level. Gabrielle's childhood memories of her father were accompanied by feelings of fear, loathing and libidinal excitation which fitted Freud's description of 'A child is being beaten' (Freud, 1919). Her father would supervise her homework in an impatient manner, shouting and sometimes hitting her with a wide belt. She recalled watching her father climb a ladder and seeing his dangling testicles. The feelings of loathing and abhorrence which she experienced at that time were then transferred onto elderly men; a transference that continues to this day.

Her father had always suffered from intestinal problems and was preoccupied with problems of food and bowel movements. Gabrielle would sometimes hear him passing wind in the toilet that was near the kitchen. In a recurrent childhood dream she slips on mud and faeces and drowns in them.

During this stage of therapy, Gabrielle's father underwent an operation for the removal of an intestinal tumour which Gabrielle vehemently claimed was benign. The oedipal threat appeared in another dream from that period: a big bull was chasing her mother and she, the little girl, hid herself in the toilet.

Gabrielle compared her relationship with her husband to that with her father, and she perceived him as a brutal man who, like her father, aroused in her both anxiety and attraction. During this phase of analysis, she frequently requested to use the toilet during and after sessions. The toilet in my office served a double function: a dirty place where she could evacuate the 'shit' in front of the therapist, and a safe place where she could hide from the phallic persecutor inside herself. Thus, therapy, at this stage, became the 'toilet-breast' (Melzer, 1967) she needed so badly.

(c) The erotised transference with its perverse undercurrents was another defence against a true therapeutic relationship. For example, Gabrielle requested my gynaecologist's address, claiming that she wanted to get rid of an ugly vaginal discharge from which she had been suffering for many years;

this conveyed her desire to touch me through my gynaecologist's hands.

Gabrielle revelled in describing her masturbatory fantasies
of being raped by a young boy who himself is forced by
older men to rape her while she is tied down. I was aware
that Gabrielle was trying to arouse my curiosity and interest
with perverse stories while at the same time checking whether
I was repelled by the manifest anal content she was exhibiting
in front of me.

Transition to a deeper level – The decision to begin analysis

My recommendation to change the form of treatment and begin
analysis aroused tremendous fear in Gabrielle of losing her old
self in the process of its being reborn. Two dreams which appeared
during this period illustrate this clearly. In the first dream Gabrielle
awoke at night, in the laboratory where she worked, wearing
only her pyjama top. She was walking along the long corridors
of the hospital which looked like a maze from which she would
not be able to escape. At first her husband and daughters were
there but afterwards she remained alone, afraid that she had lost
her way back. In her second dream Gabrielle travelled to a snow-
covered mountain. There was nobody with her on this trip. The
view was spell-binding: full of snow, ice and unmarked paths. In
the valley she saw a cemetery. As in the first dream, she felt lost,
until she suddenly saw a shadow behind her, a stranger who
helped her find her way back.

Whereas during the psychotherapy phase the anal and oedipal
levels surfaced without too much accompanying anxiety, this phase
was characterised by depression and a strong fear of madness.
Gabrielle's anxiety, connected to death wishes towards herself and
towards me as the representation of the maternal figure who is
supposed to take care of her, began to surface.

During this phase of analysis, reality and fantasy were forced
to meet as a result of an event in my own life: an emergency surgical
procedure forced me to disappear from Gabrielle's life for two weeks
with no prior preparation whatsoever. Working through this
experience afterwards in analysis brought up memories of Gabrielle
losing her mother on the operating table and her avoidance of
mourning after her mother's death. Gabrielle felt that her mother
had preferred death to a life full of suffering. She perceived me
as a 'living' mother who was able to undergo surgery and survive,

which gave her hope that she too could undergo her 'operation' – the analysis – without perishing.

Gabrielle overcame her fear of getting lost in the process and made the decision to continue the long journey ahead of her.

Phase II – The schizoid level

After her resistances on an anal and oedipal level were patiently worked through, Gabrielle felt understood and supported sufficiently to face the ultimate test of bringing the fear-ridden infant in herself into the treatment relationship. Although she was unable to let her feelings emerge plainly, it was clear that she felt she was a frightened, weak, helpless little child who had to depend on her analyst for support and protection, while at the same time fearing she would be ridiculed and rejected if she showed this openly. It was essential that she pass through this stage before facing the impact of her mother's past upon herself and upon her relationship with her own daughter.

In the transference, Gabrielle expressed her schizoid dilemma – her swinging back and forth between remoteness and closeness – both verbally and non-verbally. She would sometimes become a baby, covering herself with a blanket pulled up to her neck and referring to the piece of plastic covering the edge of the couch as 'my diaper'. At other times she would lie during the entire session with one foot on the floor, ready to jump up and escape. She expressed the desire to arrive at therapy on time, but would do everything possible in order to be late. Gabrielle moved to my town, to my very neighbourhood, in order to be close to 'analysis', but she would forget to come to sessions. She fought against her powerful need for dependency through anal struggles for control.

Gabrielle expressed oral wishes both during and outside the analytic session. After the session she would buy food for her daughters. 'A child who accepts love can also give love', she explained. In analysis, she complained of headaches and repeatedly requested a pill 'to kill the pain'. She was seeking medication from me that would enable her to conquer the painful thoughts that constantly tortured her. Her request stemmed from her wish to get food from 'the good breast' (Klein, 1932). At the same time, she perceived me as the omnipotent phallic mother who caused her physical and psychic pain. In the transference, she held me responsible for that. 'Life and death are at the mercy of psychoanalysis. I'm beginning to think that my headaches are caused by analysis; I don't know of anything else that could have upset my balance.' The pain thus had the double function of being a cry for help and a simultaneous rejection of it.

Analysis revealed Gabrielle's constant oscillation between dependence and independence, trust and distrust, acceptance and resistance to treatment, her need for a relationship which provided security and her fear that all relationships were a threat to her separate existence. Analysis was for her what Guntrip referred to as 'The In and Out Programme' (Guntrip, 1980): an unceasing attempt to break away from something that she was holding on to with all her might.

During this phase of analysis, Gabrielle was ready to relate to her father's illness. It seems that Gabrielle had known all along that her father's tumour was malignant, although she denied it. The father, aware of his dreadful condition, tried to commit suicide by swallowing a large quantity of tranquillisers and cognac. He was promptly taken to hospital where he was resuscitated but never fully recovered. Gabrielle took care of him during the last stages of his life – even helping him with his intimate bodily functions, a fact which she found libidinally arousing. She felt that returning home sexually aroused from her father's bedside was due to her confrontation with death and her wish to reaffirm life and vanquish death in an omnipotent way. In analysis she had the opportunity to work through her feelings towards her dying father, aware of the mixture of love and hatred that she felt towards him. She was also searching for the fatherly love she had lost, for the father of her childhood who, until she was six, had provided her with love and affection. At the same time, she felt that she was taking revenge on her father by caring for him so faithfully and making him totally dependent upon her. Gabrielle imagined that her care and love made him feel guilty for the things he had not given her. She projected the image of the brutal, sadistic father upon me in the transference. Seeing me wearing a wide belt during one of the sessions led Gabrielle to search in her father's attic for the belt she was hit with as a child. She found the belt and realised that it was much smaller than the one imprinted on her memory. The working-through of this memory lessened her anxiety towards me.

During the official mourning period following her father's death, she attempted, with the aid of her paternal uncles and aunts, to reconstruct her family history. She discovered that her father had had leftist leanings and that he himself had led a group of fleeing children into the forest during the Holocaust. Her father's private 'holocaust' came to light with the story of his glass eye. During a quarrel with his own father, he picked up a hammer, intending to hit him, but instead injured and destroyed his own eye. This story of violence and punishment awakened deep fear in Gabrielle.

Gabrielle's father became acquainted with his wife through a matchmaker when he was around thirty years old. Her mother had a limp as a result of her flight through the forest. Her father was considered very unattractive because of his glass eye. The marriage was obviously an encounter between two impaired persons, each carrying a burden of suffering, depression and anger which they transmitted to their offspring.

In the period following her father's death, Gabrielle expressed her feelings regarding being orphaned and her longing for me as a figure who could replace her parents. With the approach of the Jewish holidays and her birthday, Gabrielle expressed her desire for a warm, loving family, behind which lay her unconscious fantasies of rebirth.

At this painful and vulnerable juncture in her life, I had to inform Gabrielle about my impending summer holiday. I was unaware of the traumatic series of events that this forthcoming separation would trigger. Gabrielle expressed her dissatisfaction regarding the separation, but left the session without clearly acknowledging her anger towards me. Instead, she drove wildly away, did not stop at a pedestrian crossing and hit an elderly woman who was crossing the road. Gabrielle did not stop immediately, but continued driving a little further down the road and then returned to the scene, full of anger at the woman who had 'bumped into her car'. She drove the woman, who had injuries to the ribs, to the nearest hospital without feeling any guilt towards her. On her way home from the hospital, she saw a sick little kitten in the street and took it home in order to save it.

In analysis, we attempted to understand the accident in light of the therapeutic relationship. As she was apparently unable to express her anger towards me with regard to my coming holiday, she acted out her aggressive, unconscious impulses in a violent manner. The elderly woman served as my substitute, the symbol of the 'abandoning' mother whom Gabrielle was sentencing to death.

As a reaction formation to her deed, she picked up the sick little kitten, which symbolised her defective daughter as well as the little girl aspect within herself, and tried to revivify it. Gabrielle was attempting to save the little girl in herself through the act of 'killing'. In her fantasy, the defective child (herself) and the elderly woman (the mother) were linked by a magical, omnipotent link and the life of the one was tied up with the death of the other.

The attempt to understand and work through Gabrielle's behaviour in analysis was met with strong resistance. Gabrielle refused to see any connection between her aggressive wishes and the accident that 'happened' to her, and accused me of 'judging' her. Our search for the feelings that lay behind her aggressive behaviour revealed that her violent acting-out was a means of neutralising the pain, frustration and disappointment connected with our forthcoming separation. The elaborate working-through of these feelings facilitated the re-emergence of Gabrielle's superego in the form of guilt feelings. 'I'm afraid of getting my driving licence back because I'm afraid that I might kill somebody. How can we have such a deadly weapon in our hands and never think of it in such terms?'

Only later on in analysis were we able to make a connection between this accident and other accidents that had 'happened' to Gabrielle, and examine her pattern of unconsciously hurting people close to her.

Phase III – Reconstruction of the trauma and its transmission from mother to child up to the third generation

The revivification in the transference of the trauma of the original separation from her mother, which only now acquired an overt quality, helped us to uncover Gabrielle's conflicting, painful relationships with, and abandonment of, primary objects. First, Gabrielle brought up her relationship with her disturbed child.

Gabrielle told me how worried she was about her younger daughter, then thirteen years old, who seemed to be preoccupied with death and living in a fantasy world where her fear of death was intermingled with death wishes. At home, as well as in school, the child told bizarre stories about a family (father, mother and young daughter) that inhabited her throat. She described the little girl as paralysed and confined to a wheelchair. The little girl's mother took her for a walk, pushing the wheelchair ahead of her, and the wheelchair returned empty; the child had fallen out and been run over. In her story, the child was taken to hospital where nobody knew whether she would live or die. The daughter's inclination was to think that the child would die. Gabrielle agreed to the school's recommendation that a psychological reassessment of the girl be made in order to help her.

In analysis meanwhile, waiting for the results of the reassessment, Gabrielle 'flirted' more than ever with the idea of abandoning treatment. The meaning of this abandonment became clearer when, during this anxious period, Gabrielle disclosed her 'terrible secret' of abandoning the little girl during her first year of life. When her younger daughter was four months old, Gabrielle arranged to leave her with a babysitter in order to return to work. The babysitter had four children of her own; the youngest a baby himself.

Gabrielle knew that this was not an ideal environment for her daughter but eventually convinced herself that a baby requires nothing more than food and sleep. The only information that Gabrielle could provide about the baby's development at that time was that she hardly gained any weight, although no organic problem was discovered. The baby began to gain weight satisfactorily at the age of one year when Gabrielle quit her job in order to take care of her, but she did not develop normally. Gabrielle felt that her 'abandonment' of her younger daughter was the main reason for her abnormal development. She projected her harsh judgemental attitude upon me, afraid that I would judge her act and punish her with rejection and abandonment. She feared that by revealing her 'crime' she had broken our therapeutic alliance. Her constant wish to discontinue analysis at this point was an attempt to achieve active mastery over the passive trauma which threatened her. During the session in which Gabrielle informed me, in a tone devoid of emotion, of the results of her daughter's psychological report, she announced her final decision to leave analysis. The report showed that the child was cognitively retarded, very sensitive, with gaps in various developmental areas. The report also suggested that the child had suffered a terrible trauma at the age of several months. Psychological treatment was recommended, since the girl behaved in a very anxious manner.

Gabrielle vehemently maintained that her decision to leave analysis at this point was purely financial. I tried in vain to link this abandonment to the feelings of guilt and pain which the test results must have evoked in her. Gabrielle got up abruptly and left.

Gabrielle's abandonment of treatment was a difficult experience for me. I tried to analyse the thoughts and feelings which her violent acting-out evoked in me from the point of view of the therapeutic work in which we were involved, as well as by working through my needs and conflicts in this regard.

I was first preoccupied with the problem that had preceded the breaking of the therapeutic alliance. Had I made a mistake in supporting the idea of a psychological re-examination of the child which, in turn, had evoked unbearable feelings of guilt in the mother? It was very clear to me that I could not have dealt with the deterioration in the girl's situation in any other way. Discovering Gabrielle's feelings regarding this child was the only way to carry out true analysis. Gabrielle had accepted the school's recommendation that the child be re-examined, which showed that she too wanted to help her daughter, as well as the little girl inside herself. I wondered how I was supposed to treat a patient who refused to deal with the painful subject of the abandonment of her daughter. And if I hadn't taken this active role, wouldn't I have been an 'accomplice to the crime' by ignoring guilt feelings which we would not have had any chance to work through? On a different level, Gabrielle's abandonment evoked heavy feelings of guilt in me which found expression in a disturbing question: 'What did I do to her that made her leave my office in such a manner?' I later understood that this feeling was transmitted by Gabrielle through massive projective identification. Gabrielle had similar feelings towards her daughter and asked herself what she had done to inflict this permanent damage.

I also had to deal with my feelings of anger resulting from the narcissistic hurt inflicted by Gabrielle. She left analysis after undergoing a year of intensive psychotherapy and two-and-a-half years of analysis. The emotional investment in our work had been very great. By abandoning analysis, Gabrielle was attempting to destroy me as well as the treatment, without giving us a chance to work through what had happened. I began to have doubts about whether analysis was the right treatment for her. Moreover, I probed the need that I had to 'save' and 'repair', and also my feelings of omnipotence which had probably led to my decision to treat this patient by analysis.

From a different angle, the narcissistic hurt enabled me to empathise with this patient who was burdened with an impaired child. My countertransference feelings helped me to understand how such a child could wound a parent's self-esteem by serving as a constant reminder of 'failure'. I also felt the inherent frustration of this, since the child cannot provide the parent with satisfaction, despite the parent doing the utmost to bestow upon the child the 'good-enough mothering' (Winnicott, 1965) needed for this purpose.

On another level, I realised that to let Gabrielle go without clarifying what had happened would be to play into her magical, omnipotent fantasy of the 'murderess-mother' – a mother who abandons and thus causes permanent damage.

In her relationship with me, Gabrielle would either destroy me by her abandonment – the way she imagined she had left her daughter – or I would destroy her by imposing a heavy burden of guilt on her and letting her bear it alone. I therefore decided that it was necessary to show her that even if she rejected me, I would 'survive', and that she should not destroy our therapeutic relationship without giving us a chance to save it (Winnicott, 1971).

Thus, after a period of ten days, I wrote to Gabrielle and invited her to my office in order to clarify the reasons for her leaving so abruptly. She accepted my suggestion that we continue therapy, and during the next three sessions, in which she explored her feelings regarding the traumatic event of 'abandoning' treatment, we were able to rebuild the therapeutic alliance which has remained sound ever since. Gabrielle explained that she experienced leaving analysis as my abandonment of her at a critical point in her life. Only after leaving did she realise how overburdened she was by guilt; a feeling of guilt towards her child had accompanied her throughout the years, but only now did it 'come to light' and she could no longer deny it. She was sure that I held her responsible for her daughter's psychological condition. Her anger towards me stemmed from the fact that I had let her leave analysis feeling so guilty. 'That was no way to end treatment', she said. Only after she returned to analysis were we able to understand, on a deeper level, the trauma of her abandoning her younger daughter as well as her own abandonment by her mother.

During this phase we began exploring Gabrielle's fear regarding the very special bond that existed between the child and herself. 'I think that she feels what I feel, and in a way she reads my thoughts.' I became aware that there might be a symbiotic relationship between Gabrielle and her daughter, and that, through the child, the mother might be expressing feelings that she was unaware of. It was possible that the child, identifying with the aggressive, destructive aspects of her mother, was expressing through her behaviour and stories, suicidal tendencies which actually belonged to the mother and not to the child herself. This hypothesis was confirmed by the following occurrences:

(a)   A long series of suicidal dreams in which Gabrielle expressed
      her fear of death, intermingled with death wishes towards
      her daughter but seldom towards herself.
          In Gabrielle's dreams, the girl is run over by a car, or
      drowns. Gabrielle warned her to be careful because she felt
      that the child was fulfilling her inner wish to disappear. For
      example: 'I dreamt a dream in which Tali, my little daughter,
      was run over by a car. There was a car full of children and
      she fell out of it. I was totally overwhelmed, and by the time
      I reacted, another car came and ran her over.' In the associ-
      ations related to this dream she said: 'This morning I was
      watching from the window as Tali crossed the road. Suddenly,
      I saw a car approaching and I became terribly frightened. I
      wondered what would have happened had she been run
      over by it? At the same time I thought that perhaps my life
      would be easier.'
(b)   A process of identification (fusion) with me in the transference.
      Gabrielle became confused about her own identity and was
      incapable of differentiating between who she is and who I
      am. For example, she thought that she saw me walking
      around the neighbourhood dressed provocatively, and then
      she suddenly realised that those were actually her own
      clothes that she had recently worn.

This confusion of identities, which lasted for quite a long period
in analysis, pointed to the possibility that a similar process had
taken place between herself and her own mother during an early
stage in Gabrielle's development. I would like to illustrate this
theme by an excerpt from analysis (I = Ilany; G = Gabrielle):

G: Last night I dreamt about you. In the dream you looked
     totally different – short black hair, a small face. I was surprised
     how much you had changed. You were sitting silently and
     reacted only with facial expressions. Suddenly, you changed
     back into your regular self. I felt very anxious – how could I
     have seen somebody else and then it's you? It's like insanity;
     I've lost control.
I: The image in the dream – who does she remind you of?
G: A girl I saw a short time ago at the university. A small face;
     a fine, small mouth. In the dream, I felt as if it were me. It's
     as if I identified with you; you and I were interchanging and
     this frightened me. Consciously I don't want you to resemble
     me and I don't want to look like you. The woman in the dream

reminded me of a supervisor in a laboratory where I once worked, a serious woman, good-looking for her age. There was something in the supervisor's face which reminded me of my mother. It's as if I'm looking for my mother in everybody. You don't remind me of my mother, either in the way you look or in your behaviour, but maybe there are things I'm not aware of. The woman in my dream reminded me of my mother.

I: In your dream I change into a woman who reminded you of your mother.

G: Yesterday my eldest daughter asked me a question related to a book she was reading – 'What kind of animal would you like to be?' I told her, 'A little chick.' She said, 'What? A chick who is so dependent and can't do anything by itself?' Just see what I wanted to be – I wanted to be cared for and spoiled.

I: You want me to care for you, you want to be my spoiled little chick. You therefore changed me into a woman who resembles your mother.

G: Yes, the face of the woman in my dream was a mixture of my face and my mother's. I have another association. You'll lick your lips when you hear it. The girl in the dream – she reminded me of a movie star who acts in westerns, the whore who owns the pub.

I: Why should I lick my lips?

G: Because there is something sexual in this. The girl in the dream seems to be a good soul, but she's also cheap. Yesterday I heard a lecture about frightening things, like homosexuality, for example.

I: I think you're hinting that you feel sexually attracted to the woman who appeared in your dream – namely, to me.

G: Yes, that's true, what you've just said. Sometimes there are young women with whom I think I could have an affair if I were a man. I am not always so open. If you had looked like the woman in my dream, I would have been attracted to you. I told you once about my husband who flirted with all my women friends. I chose good-looking ones. When I was twenty, I saw the movie *Sister George*. This was the first movie about lesbians I'd ever seen. It aroused me, and I became anxious. I read afterwards that every woman has a lesbian aspect, every man has a homosexual one, and I became more aware of that in me. When I feel at ease with a woman, I want to touch her.

I: I hear you telling me how much you want to touch me.
G: In my dream I became frightened, because I understood that
     the person I was talking to was you. But the most terrifying
     thing for me was to see you as the whore from the movies,
     since I saw myself in her image. And that's absurd, since she
     seemed to be gentle and pretty, but she reminded me of a
     cheap woman, of myself and my mother.

Thus we discovered that, in addition to her homosexual attraction
towards me, Gabrielle saw herself and me (or herself and her
mother) fused into one image that was reflected in her dream.
This image which she discovered in herself contained two aspects:
on the one hand, she had beauty and tenderness, and, on the other
hand, she was driven by a 'cheap' passion.

At the start of analysis Gabrielle said very little about her
mother, only mentioning *en passant* her plight during the
Holocaust and her mother's story about surviving by fleeing
through the forest (her first 'Mythos of Survival'[2] [Klein, 1981]).
The story recounted her mother's encounter with a German
soldier who kicked her in the foot, leaving her permanently
crippled.

During puberty, Gabrielle read extensively about the Holocaust,
which aroused sadistic fantasies in her about what had happened
to her mother in the above encounter. Her unconscious translated
the brutal act of kicking into an act of sexual abuse, and she
imagined that her mother had been raped by German soldiers in
her flight through the forest. Gabrielle connected her sadistic masturbatory fantasies to what she referred to as 'my Nazi period'.
She saw herself as attracted to the Aryan type of man whom she
described as 'blond and blue-eyed, cruel and violent'.

The wish to be raped by me in analysis was expressed in the
transference. 'I am attracted to force, mainly intellectual force; I
want you to shake me in some way so that I can really change. I
know you can do it, you've inserted painful things into my head
already.' On the other hand, she tried very hard to trap me and
turn me into her 'victim' by making repetitive, aggressive demands
on me to fulfil her wishes (such as changing appointment times,
postponing payments or trying to obtain feedback about herself).
If she felt I was agreeing to one of her requests she would celebrate
her 'little victory' over me.

The way in which Gabrielle identified with her mother's experiences now became apparent. She identified, on the one hand,

with the role of the victim who had been sadistically raped and abused, and, on the other hand, with the violent, brutal aggressor who aroused her own sadistic fantasies.

In my feelings of countertransference, I felt I was involved in a sado-masochistic relationship in which I was assigned alternately the roles of aggressor and victim.

Only at this stage of treatment did Gabrielle become aware of the impact of her mother's past upon her. The dreams and stories about the Holocaust that appeared now in analysis described trauma which, historically, did not belong to her own past, but to her mother's. She had been completely engulfed by her mother's feelings and was unable to differentiate between herself and her mother. Gabrielle described situations in her childhood in which identification with her mother was total, such as the time when she, together with other schoolchildren, was required to sing a song at a school performance. When her turn came, she suddenly sang a Yiddish song, a song that cried for help in a helpless situation, which her mother often sang – 'Es brennt, briderlech, es brennt' (Gebirtig, 1937) – without knowing why she did this.

Gabrielle's illusion that she had been with her mother even before her own birth (Klein, 1973a) was based on her dreams, fantasies and acting out.

It appeared that the depressed, sick mother did not see her husband as a partner with whom she could share her grief; she used her daughter instead as a person to whom she could convey traces of her experiences, either narratively or by acting out. Gabrielle herself confirmed this in the process of working through her feelings towards her mother. 'My black feelings, where do they come from? I know they come from my mother. Not because of her illness, but because of the war she went through. She transmitted her depression to me, her sad face was always before me, the feeling of unhappiness, the quiet despair.' By identifying totally with her mother, the mother's traumatic past as well as her guilt of survival became her own.

In analysis, Gabrielle recollected another story about her mother's survival (her second 'Mythos of Survival'): 'Mother suffered terrible things, she ran away and left her entire family behind. I very much admire her wish to survive; I wouldn't have had the desire to live any more.' She told me that she tried to commit suicide twice, and when she put the rope around her neck she saw her mother's face telling her, 'If you've lived up until now, you have to go on living for everybody else.'

Here we see the mother's polarised roles – that of the 'murderess', who feels guilty about 'murdering' her relatives whom she was unable to save from destruction, and the 'saviour', the mother who gives the order to go on living.

Gabrielle's identification with the 'murderess' mother was expressed in analysis in her recurrent dreams about the Holocaust, in which the main theme was her running through the forest and saving herself while leaving her two daughters, or the little one, behind in peril of death. Gabrielle revealed her guilt about not being able to save her mother from the Holocaust or from her illness and depression. She felt guilty about being unable to save her younger daughter from her destiny of being emotionally disturbed. On another level, she felt guilty for surviving at all, when so many others had perished.

The identification with the 'murderess' mother was also expressed in the theme of having to choose between two children: one that would live and the other that would die (connected with stories she had read and the movie *Sophie's Choice*). On one level, we understood this as her conflicting wishes of keeping her healthy child and getting rid of the problematic one. On a deeper level, there was the identification with the mother's double message which enjoined her simultaneously to stay alive and to die.

Gabrielle felt she wanted to save her little daughter as well as be rid of her. She also felt that she wanted to cure the little girl within herself, and also to kill her.

Phase IV – Construction of the self

During the last phase of analysis, we dealt with two main issues:

1. The reconstruction of Gabrielle's childhood, which led to changes in her relationship with the representation of internal objects and eventually to changes towards external objects and the world as a whole.
2. The construction of Gabrielle's self, which consisted of: (a) Gabrielle's internalisation of the analyst's supportive and hopeful image, which brought about positive changes in her perception of her self and which rebuilt her faith in the future; and (b) experiencing the birth of a new self in analysis.

This phase began with Gabrielle's desire to find out more about her childhood. Gabrielle learned that her mother had been unable to take care of her after her birth because of the deterioration of her own health. Gabrielle was cared for by her paternal grandmother, a silent soul, disconnected from reality and from relationships with people, who lived in a world of her own. Another important emotional detail which she learned was that her mother had written songs about her childhood in the ghetto. With the working-through of her history, Gabrielle's relationship to the inner representation of her mother changed. She felt less guilty towards her, and also felt an increased emotional closeness to her.

Gabrielle became less frightened of her passive, dependent needs. When I interpreted her longing to be my baby in treatment as her desire to be taken care of by me, she was able to accept this without resistance. I will illustrate this with an excerpt from analysis:

G: Today I woke up early, since I had an examination at the university. I found a white piece of paper on my desk and on it was written, 'To Mother, Good Luck!' My big girl, she understands me. I was so moved, she had decorated it with beautiful letters. This girl gives me a lot emotionally. I don't know why, maybe it's connected to her infancy. If there's something that I long for, it's the first five years that we had together. It gave me so much satisfaction then. I raised that girl according to Dr. Spock's advice, feeding her every four hours, boundaries, love.

I: I think you're hinting that the way you raised your daughter is similar to analysis – the five years that we've spent together, four hours every week, and the emotional acceptance within a framework of clear boundaries.

G: (laughing) It really is similar. My daughter now returns the love she received from me throughout the years. How do you express the warm feeling you have towards somebody? Through giving! That is the most beautiful way. Things look different to me now. The same with you, the fact that I see the beauty in you is not recent, it began when we had that crisis. Obviously you haven't changed, but you seem different to me.

I: I feel that you're now bestowing on me the warm feelings which you feel I've invested in you over the years.

The strengthening of Gabrielle's self, which can be seen in her ability to accept her own frailties, was expressed in a change in her relationship with her daughter, which may also be perceived as a change towards the impaired aspect of her self: 'I'm able to appreciate my child's beauty now because something's changed in me. Something in my own perception of myself and her. I'm more at peace with the good and bad things in myself.'

The change in Gabrielle's relationship with internal and external objects was linked to changes in her relationship with her self. This change was expressed in the transference in her relationship with me. 'For years I didn't know whether analysis was good or bad for me. Now I know what analysis did for me. I'm less afraid of people, less afraid to believe in them. I'm still not totally sure of myself, and I don't know if my judgement or intuition are always right, but even if they're not, nothing terrible will happen. I've gained a lot from you and I'd like to be able to reciprocate it.'

The change in Gabrielle's relationship with me sprang from the growth of a new, more mature self, capable of relating to another individual as a separate person. The psychic 'frost', the purpose of which was to defend Gabrielle against the threat of a world full of animosity, had almost melted: 'Once I was a very closed person', said Gabrielle. 'I no longer see people as threatening and I'm able to reveal my feelings.'

Following this, a childhood memory brought us back to the beginning of our analytic journey, the trip through the 'ice castle'. As a child, Gabrielle referred to her parents' home as the 'ice castle' because it was very cold. She had frequently suffered from cold sores on her hands and legs, which she wrapped in 'stinking bandages'. In analysis, we understood the stinking bandages to be defences which served to protect her damaged skin against the pain caused by contact with the external world. While telling me about the 'ice castle', Gabrielle complained of a feeling of numbness in her hands, as if they were frozen. She reacted to this spontaneously. 'I won't let myself freeze. Now I know that when I came to treatment I was suffering mostly from fear that I would freeze. Today I don't have this fear and I don't want to freeze.' I realised that Gabrielle was still afraid of her wish to become numb, but compared with the past, she was now aware of it and prepared to fight it with all her might.

Another dominant aspect of this phase of treatment was Gabrielle's construction of a sense of future. Apparently her fixation on her mother's traumatic past had made a sense of a future in a safer world impossible for her. The reconstruction of her history and childhood, the lessening of her deep fears and the revivification of her frozen ability to feel as a result of deep analytic regression, gave her the ability to think about the past and the future simultaneously. Gabrielle related this to her internalisation of me as a source of hope. 'You have encouraged me, you've given me the feeling that treatment holds a future for me, that life holds a future for me. I now feel I have more courage than I had before. Now your words reverberate in my head, I think I appreciate myself 50 per cent more because of you.'

Gabrielle's wish for the birth of a new self, apparent from her first dream in treatment, reappeared more emphatically during this phase. In her dreams, Gabrielle described the birth of two aspects of her own self through the birth of her two daughters. 'I dreamt that my younger daughter was walking in water. The water was full of vegetation. It reminded me a lot of birth, of coming out of the vagina, hair surrounding it. I was dreaming that my child was born. It wasn't a frightening dream this time, she wasn't going to drown.' Another time, the dream was about the older girl. 'There was a channel full of dirty water, rain water. My older daughter went in until she couldn't stand, and then she got out. I was waiting for her.'

Gabrielle's wish for the birth of a new self that appeared in her dreams was also apparent in her description of images which symbolised new internal structures. Gabrielle described her feelings when, leaving one of her analytic sessions, she discovered a new house on the street which she hadn't noticed before. She later dreamt that she was looking through the window of her apartment and saw a wonderful view, a blue sky and the shadow of a snow-covered mountain, on top of which stood an ancient structure. Contrary to her dream at the beginning of analysis in which her walk on a snow-covered mountain was accompanied by her anxiety of getting lost, she now looked out at the view from inside her own flat, from an inner house, with the cold, frozen aspect remaining on the outside.

Discussion

This analysis can be viewed as two concentric circles whose common centre is the transmission of trauma. The outermost circle consists of a manifest layer of defences, such as the evacuation of anal material overlaid with overt oedipal wishes and fantasies. The transference on this level was erotic with perverse undercurrents and was used as a defence against a true therapeutic relationship.

Exploration of the manifest level led us to the inner circle, a deeper layer of the personality which was characterised by the patient's struggle to retain her sense of self. Here we discovered a fantasised inner world full of internal bad objects and object-splitting. The relationship with me during this period had a schizoid quality, swinging back and forth between remoteness and closeness. The patient's self was not strongly integrated, and thus its capacity to enter into a good relationship with me was impaired, yet it could not be left alone without anxiety and insecurity. Because of my impression that the acute difficulty lay in the patient's undifferentiated self, we began to search for its origin. We first uncovered the patient's symbiotic relationship with her younger daughter and her inability to achieve self-differentiation. This unusual relationship, and the kind of relationship (fusion) which developed towards me in the transference during this phase of analysis, led us to investigate the patient's relationship with her maternal object. At the heart of the patient's undiffer-entiated self we discovered the transmission of trauma from mother to daughter during two consecutive generations. I would like now to explore the pattern of trauma which was transmit-ted from one generation to another:

1. *Traumatisation through loss of one's separate sense of self.* Gabrielle was exposed to her mother's severe traumatisation very early in life, at a stage in which the introjection–projection mechanism is dominant. She therefore experienced her mother's traumati-sation almost as though it had happened to herself because she was totally absorbed in her mother's feelings at a time when she lacked an adult's ability to organise, conceptualise and articulate this kind of traumatisation.

We found that, in both generations, the trauma was transmit-ted through unconscious processes of identification, and the mother's inability to help her daughter achieve self–object dif-ferentiation. The daughter, as a result, felt the need to live in her mother's past (Kestenberg, 1980; Auerhahn and Prelinger, 1983).

2. *Traumatisation by the child being exploited as a life-saving device.* The traumatisation in both generations consisted of uncon-sciously using the child as a vehicle for repetition of the trauma. Since the aggressive, destructive aspects connected with her own traumatisation endangered the mother's own physical and psychic survival, they were projected upon the child who was thus used unconsciously as a life-saving device.

3. *Traumatisation by abandonment of the child.* Birth and abandonment were linked together in Gabrielle's life. She was first abandoned by her mother after her birth, and later abandoned by her for ever when she was about to give birth to her older daughter. Gabrielle's abandonment of her own child during her first year of life was the outcome of the mechanic of repetition-compulsion connected to her own experiences in life.

The incident that led us to explore the trauma of abandonment was the impending separation for a summer holiday at a most vulnerable point in analysis. The original separation was thus revivified and acquired traumatic meaning in the transference.

Gabrielle's abandonment as a baby, which was reconstructed by her in analysis, was due to the deterioration of her mother's health following Gabrielle's birth. It is very possible that her mother's poor physical and psychological condition during the first year after her delivery did not allow her to provide her child with the necessary 'good-enough mothering' (Winnicott, 1965). This trauma of abandonment in the first year of life was repeated in Gabrielle's relationship with her younger daughter. The reasons that she was unable to raise this child, in contrast to her firstborn, were manifold. For example: (a) this child was the representation of narcissistic hurt. She probably had some organic birth defect, which represented to Gabrielle the defective part in herself which she badly wanted to get rid of; and (b) the child was the representation of Gabrielle's lack of hope. Gabrielle felt that she could be a mother to her older daughter since she was blonde and blue-eyed, the 'Aryan' type who had a chance to survive. The impaired younger one, who resembled her own mother, was sentenced, in her mind, to death and destruction. Therefore there was no point in trying to save her.

4. *Traumatisation of the child by erasing the possibility of hope and of a future.* The story of the mother's traumatisation – her encounter with the German soldier who kicked her in the foot, permanently crippling her – was a story of physical injury and evil. The mother, who should have been a messenger of hope, was identified by the child with the traumatic message that she herself conveyed. The implication of this story for the child was that the world was an evil, unsafe place, full of pain and suffering, without hope or future.

One of the aims of therapy in this case was to facilitate the differentiation between the mother's experiences and the patient's infantile fantasies about destruction and loss. Gabrielle's increased ability to distinguish between internal and external reality in matters connected with her mother's traumatisation enhanced her capacity to differentiate between present and past, without which there could be no concept of future (Grubrich-Simitis, 1984).

The object representation of the mother as a murderess and a saviour changed, making her appear less omnipotent and dangerous to her daughter. As a result of this, Gabrielle felt less guilty towards her own problematic child and less destructive towards herself. The daughter, who is undergoing treatment herself, is now living in a safer world, is able to express anger in a more verbal way, and consequently her suicidal thoughts are disappearing.

II Death in an Embrace of Love[3]

> *'The confrontation with death – and the reprieve from it – makes*
> *everything look so precious, so sacred, so beautiful that I feel more*
> *strongly than ever the impulse to love it, to embrace it, and to let*
> *myself be overwhelmed by it ... Death, and its ever present pos-*
> *sibility makes love, passionate love, more possible. I wonder if we*
> *could love passionately, if ecstasy would be possible at all, if we*
> *knew we'd never die.'*
>
> From a letter by Abraham Maslow

This chapter describes the theme of differentiation and growth
in the third analysis of an 'interminable' analytic process. (This
analysis was preceded by two earlier ones.) The patient is the
daughter of a Jewish, American-born mother and a Holocaust-
survivor father, whose previous wife and child had perished in
the Holocaust. The patient's first encounter with analysis was in
the US at the age of twelve, with the onset of anorexic symptoms;
she sought analysis again when aged twenty-one and underwent
treatment for nine years. The patient terminated that analysis to
emigrate to Israel, where she became the focus of a psychoanalytic paper (Kestenberg, 1982). In Israel she was in analysis with
me for five years, in the course of which we dealt mainly with
the patient's process of differentiation from primary object representations and the strengthening of her own identity. The first
part of analysis revolved around her separation from her father's
traumatic past. We achieved this by working through the transference relationship in relation to two themes: (a) the father's secret
(the loss of his first family during the Holocaust), which the
patient discovered shortly before terminating her previous analysis
in the US; and (b) her defensive use of the Holocaust. During this
analysis, the patient's boyfriend died of a heart attack while they
were making love. The elaboration of this traumatic event allowed

the patient to reactivate and rework her sado-masochistic fantasies linked to her father's first family.

The latter part of this analysis dealt with furthering the patient's process of individuation by working through her relationship with her mother. The patient's reconstruction of a separate self and her ability to build a life of her own led us to terminate analysis.

Case History

Rachel is the eldest of three children. The atmosphere in her home was imbued with depression and guilt. Rachel's father had kept the loss of his first family secret from his second wife and children. He never spoke about his losses and injuries, but worked hard and advanced himself in their community. He looked down on his wife, who acted as his shadow and considered him a hero. The wife developed a special relationship with Rachel, whom she regarded as her twin sister from whom she had great difficulty separating.

Rachel had always felt like a 'paper doll', an inanimate toy in the hands of her parents who manipulated her life according to their own wishes. The onset of anorexic symptoms at the age of twelve was caused by: (a) Rachel's living in a fantasy world belonging to her father's traumatic past (she toyed with the idea of conquering death by attempting to starve herself and survive, like the people who had survived the concentration camps); and (b) Rachel's deep anger and disdain towards her mother, with whom she had a symbiotic relationship. By not eating, Rachel was not only rejecting the cold, frustrating mother who was unable to feed her emotionally, but also was fulfilling unconsciously the mother's desire to diet. The lack of differentiation between mother and daughter was expressed through the mother's approval of her 'diets' and her constant checking of her own weight while the girl starved herself. When Rachel's condition became serious, a doctor – a friend of the family – intervened and Rachel was referred first for medical observation and then for psychiatric care. Her parents ended her analysis after one year, when her symptoms subsided.

Rachel entered analysis again at the age of twenty-one. She sought out her previous analyst who had helped her during childhood and from whom she had been prematurely torn away by her parents. Her complaints revolved around bodily functions, interpersonal relationships and impaired performance (Kestenberg, 1982).

Just before terminating analysis in order to come to Israel, Rachel learned of her father's former family from a relative who had been with him during the Holocaust. Following this discovery, she entered into a state of shock, lost her way to her car which was parked in a nearby parking lot, then fell off the steps of the bus she had taken home and was almost hit by a passing vehicle. Despite her psychic distress, she decided to terminate analysis as planned.

Here in Israel, Rachel fell in love with a painter on the verge of divorce, the father of a two-year-old child whom he had left abroad with his mother. The relationship had a sado-masochistic quality and ended abruptly. Abandoned and rejected, Rachel felt that her world was falling apart. She was very depressed, unable to cope with life, and suffered an attack of derealisation. Rachel felt that she needed analysis in order to survive and thus sought professional help. She was referred to me through her former analyst's colleagues in Israel.

The elaboration of the father's secret

Rachel threw herself into analysis five times a week with a 'loyalty' I have seldom seen. She conveyed the urgency of her needs by giving me the feeling that analysis was vital to her existence.

I gradually became aware that Rachel was treating me like a life-saving device, alternately clinging to me for survival and pushing me away when she felt safe. In Rachel's words, I was 'a blanket to wrap myself with when I am freezing', an object which could be discarded after use. Only later in analysis were we able to understand that this behaviour was a reflection of her relationship with her internal primary objects.

In the first phase of analysis we attempted to work through Rachel's feelings of guilt, envy, and her oedipal strivings which the revelation of her father's secret evoked in her.

On the basis of Rachel's conscious and unconscious fantasies, we understood that her unhappy love affair was an attempt to act out the roles in the drama of her father's past. In that relationship, she was her own father, his wife, and his child, and she assigned complementary roles to me in the transference relationship. Rachel described her fantasy that, by coming to Israel at the same age that her father left Europe, she was fulfilling her wish of becoming identical to him. She felt that he had had to mobilise all of his emotional resources in order to rebuild his life after the loss of his wife and child. In her imagination, she too had to undergo the loss of a potential family (through the loss of her lover and his child) in order to build herself anew.

The same episode also served to express her oedipal longings. By choosing a man who left his wife and small child in a faraway country, Rachel was recreating her father's past in her own life. In this way she tried to become her father's partner and give him comfort. Failing in this project, she felt hurt and rejected and wanted to die, unconsciously playing the role of the father's first wife.

Rachel experienced her father's secret as a narcissistic hurt. She now viewed herself as a 'replacement child'. Having lost her place as her father's oldest child, she felt 'squashed' between the dead child and her younger siblings. On the other hand, she felt that she now understood something she had always intuitively known, that her father could never give of himself completely to his second wife and children because part of him remained with his lost family. She claimed that a special bond existed between her father and herself; she felt that somehow she had always shared her father's secret without having ever really known it.

Rachel was torn by conflicting wishes. On the one hand, she wished to become her lover's wife but, on the other hand, she imagined reuniting him with his estranged wife and child. By so doing, she was prepared to give up her oedipal longings and play the role of being her father's child again, bringing him happiness by restoring his lost objects.

Through the transference relationship Rachel assigned me different roles. The first role can be illustrated by an episode from Eli Wiesel's story, *The Accident* (Wiesel, 1961), which she told in a session. In this episode a young doctor asks his patient who refuses to recover from his wounds, 'Why don't you want to live?' The doctor, who had always been his patient's ally against death, in this case has to fight death, against his patient's wishes. In the transference we understood Rachel's desire that I become the doctor who saves her from her own destructive tendencies. Rachel subsequently viewed me as a replacement for her sister with whom she had a very close emotional relationship. Rachel perceived me as similar to her sister in age as well as appearance. This sister had suffered a very serious illness and survived. Through her image, Rachel projected qualities of strength and uniqueness upon me which belonged to her own ideal self.

On an unconscious level, Rachel sought the image of her father's young, beloved wife in me. In her fantasies, Rachel had come to Israel to search for her. Since the woman had disappeared without burial or tombstone, Rachel believed she might have survived the Holocaust and come to Israel. Rachel described her as an ideal mother, feminine, clever and far superior to her own mother. She sometimes toyed with the idea that this woman might actually have been her real mother. Rachel imagined that her father's wife was about my age when she disappeared. She felt that I was the survivor type and that I would certainly have survived. She expressed the desire to learn from me, as from this ideal mother, the secrets of femininity, which she felt she lacked.

By working through her oedipal longings, as well as her guilt and envy connected to her father and his first family, Rachel was able to conquer the disappointment caused by her lover's abandonment. She became aware that that relationship hadn't begun to fulfil her real needs as a young woman living in the present world. This opened the way for the search for a new, different relationship.

I will now explore Rachel's sado-masochistic tendencies and guilt feelings as expressed in the transference relationship. Lurking behind her conscious wish to turn me into a saviour was Rachel's hidden, aggressive wish to become my persecutor. Her oral and anal sadistic wishes towards me in the transference were expressed through fantasies and dreams.

Rachel perceived herself as poisonous to those who love her. Her self-image was that of a porcupine – 'whoever gets stuck, gets hurt'. She recollected her affair with a man who became insane and was institutionalised after she left him. In the transference, Rachel was afraid that her ambivalence towards me would endanger my sanity.

Rachel the 'murderess/victim' appeared in the following dream: 'I was in a car, at the street corner. The car stopped. Suddenly someone was lying in the street, his head on the wheel. I could see that it was a disconnected head. Someone came and picked it up.' In her associations, Rachel first referred to herself as the victim: 'My head and heart are definitely split.' She bestowed upon me the omnipotent ability to pick up her 'severed head' and, by means of analysis, 'put her together'. But, at the same time, she was afraid of destroying me by her hostile, aggressive wishes. In her associations regarding the dream she felt that she was the historical Salome who demanded that her lover be beheaded. In the transference I felt she was asking for my head. I thus became aware of Rachel's unconscious wish to avenge her frustrated strivings for total fusion with me, which she was unable to realise in analysis.

Erotisation of death was another aspect of Rachel's sado-masochistic fantasies. This can be illustrated by a recollection from her childhood of touching and looking at death, accompanied by libidinal excitation. When she was a child, she found a dead squirrel in the driveway. She buried it, then some time later, thinking about the worms in the area, dug it up and reburied it. During analysis, she became quite excited when describing the foul smell and the rottenness of the dead squirrel. 'Maybe I wanted to see death', she said, 'like your flesh is crawling, like you're terrified'.

An incident which occurred the week before the actual trauma showed how Rachel's constant preoccupation with death was connected to her identification with the roles of victim/killer. Rachel had recently adopted a kitten, which served as a substitute child for her. Since Rachel was planning to be out of town for a day, she cancelled her analytic session then locked the kitten in the bathroom and left the heater on so it wouldn't be cold. When she returned, she found the animal lying dead near the heater. Rachel thought that since the kitten had recently suffered from diarrhoea, it had died of dehydration from the heat. She buried it, thinking of the many soldiers who had died in battles. That night, she forgot to turn off the gas heater in her living room. She woke up the next morning to a strong smell which made her aware that the gas had been on all night.

We attempted to understand this morbid episode through the transference relationship in view of the impact of her father's traumatic past. Rachel identified with the kitten who was desperately searching for warmth. When I wasn't there for her she burnt herself and dehydrated to death, thus becoming my 'victim'. At the same time, she was also the 'murderess' who killed the baby inside herself by putting it into the furnace. In this role, she was punishing herself by dying in the gas chamber, like those who died in concentration camps.

In the transference, Rachel perceived me as a source of warmth and protection (the heater), as well as destruction. Thus, when separated from me, she felt totally insecure and lost but, when reunited, she felt swallowed, absorbed and threatened by the loss of her individuality. Only later on in analysis were we able to understand this mode of relating to me against the background of her relationship with her mother.

The risk of losing both her object and herself in various ways in an intimate relationship became even more frightening when it moved from the level of fantasy to traumatic reality, when her worst fantasies regarding death were realised through the act of love.

Death in the embrace of love

During my summer vacation, Rachel became involved in a love relationship, thus giving up casual sex with no emotional involvement. This new relationship lacked the sado-masochistic quality which characterised her former relationships. She described her boyfriend as a warm, giving person who made her feel worthy of his love. She was looking for the warmth, understanding and acceptance that she received in analysis, her underlying wish being to have me in her external world. In spite of her great thirst for love, she was incapable of reciprocating her boyfriend's affection without ambivalence. She felt that her boyfriend did not fit into her outer world, that he was not up to her family's standards. She claimed that she needed him only for comfort, but in order to 'enjoy' life she needed a different partner. To need love meant to be weak, and she therefore toyed with the idea of leaving him. 'It is addictive to be loved', said Rachel, 'and it makes you weak and dependent. Whoever gets weak, can get killed.'

In her inner reality, her boyfriend, Jacob, played some very important roles. He represented her older brother (the dead child), who would have been his age had he lived. Since Jacob was caring and warm, she also related to him as a parental figure, different from her internal parental objects.

The following is a detailed description of the traumatic event that occurred after Rachel had spent a year in analysis. At seven o'clock in the morning, Rachel called and informed me that she was unable to attend her regular session that morning, but that she must see me urgently some time during the day. In answer to my enquiry about what happened, she replied in a strange voice, 'Jacob died last night.'

I saw Rachel that evening. She looked like a ghost, her face thin and pale, her eyes terribly swollen. Thanking me for agreeing to see her that same day, she asked to sit in a chair and not lie on the couch as usual. Her first words were, 'I wanted to see you because I think I killed him, like I killed the cat.'

She related the following story in a neutral voice, devoid of emotion. Rachel had spent the evening with Jacob, after not seeing him for several days. It was a quiet evening, he prepared food for both of them, she hugged him in the kitchen. As on many other occasions, they watched television and she fell asleep on his lap. Afterwards they went to bed together. He began making love to her and said, 'I've been waiting so long for this.' After a moment she felt that he was no longer inside her. Her first thought was that he had lost his erection, since this had happened occasionally. He gasped, turned over on his back and didn't move. She stroked his face and, thinking of a friend's baby who sometimes lost its breath while crying, tried to comfort him by saying, 'Relax, baby, relax!' Since he didn't react, she rocked him forcefully and he turned blue. Then she became terrified, began screaming, 'Help, police, ambulance!' and banged on the door of neighbours who hesitated to come out. Other neighbours appeared and two men tried to resuscitate Jacob with artificial respiration. After what seemed like an eternity, but was only about five minutes, an ambulance arrived. When she gathered the courage to ask what had happened to Jacob, she was told that he had died. She didn't remember what happened next. She was told that she wouldn't let go of his body, and kept screaming, 'Jacob, no! Jacob, no!' She was given a shot and awoke in hospital. At four o'clock in the morning she called a friend to drive her home, and three hours later she called me.

When she finished her story, we both sat very quietly for some time. Rachel then asked if I thought that Jacob had died of a heart attack, which was the official diagnosis. She felt she might have caused him too much excitement, since she hadn't seen him for several days. She thought that he probably could no longer bear the yes/no relationship she had created. A former boyfriend had become insane and wanted to commit suicide, and now she had killed Jacob. Whoever loved her got killed.

Listening to Rachel's story I was first overwhelmed by its content and by the unspeakable terror which accompanied it. For a short while I felt frightened and helpless. Then, I became aware that these must have been Rachel's feelings too when confronting her lover's death. I understood that her request to face me during this session was to make sure that I was alive and well. Becoming fully aware of her tremendous guilt feelings and of the danger of her becoming convinced that she really was a murderess, I decided to point out to her the other polarity of hate: namely, love. I reminded Rachel that she had given Jacob much love and affection, and that he had died a graceful death in her arms. Death, which can be so agonising and lonely, occurred to him in an embrace during the act of love. His death resembled his birth – he was born from a woman and died, in the midst of love, inside one.

There was a moment of silence, of self-reflection and discovery. Rachel looked at me and her face lit up. She remembered now that when she was informed of Jacob's death she had felt like jumping out of the window; then, recalling her appointment with me the next morning, she decided she couldn't do that. 'Anyway, it wasn't high enough', she added with a smile. At this point, we embarked on the long, arduous journey of working through the trauma Rachel had experienced during those few dramatic moments.

Working through the actual trauma

Using me as an internal good object, Rachel's first decision following the trauma was to live. She projected upon me that part of herself that fought her helplessness and depression, and found in me a source of strength which gave her courage in her battle with her guilt and her self-punishing tendencies.

Two sessions after the traumatic occurrence, Rachel asked to return to the couch, in order to bring things 'back to normal'. She expressed her wish to leave analysis, in order to avoid confronting her own pain and guilt. She also conveyed that she did not believe in my ability to contain her suffering. Working through her inability to trust me convinced her that she had an ally in me, and was therefore not alone in her struggle for life. Only then did she decide to stay. She reminded herself often of my interpretation of her lover's death in her arms, which helped her undo her belief that she was a murderess. 'Before I came here I kept thinking that I killed him, and I couldn't live with that. Your words made me look at the whole picture in a different light. And also, it's too grandiose to think that I could have killed him.'

Rachel conquered her wish to run away from analysis during this critical period. In contrast to the guilt she had felt in the past, which meant weakness since it stemmed from her identification with her father's helplessness in the Holocaust, she felt stronger and assumed responsibility for her life and well-being. This feeling enabled us to work through the way she exploited the Holocaust as a defence, using it to represent her own destructive wishes which she was not in touch with. Rachel became aware that the world

of the six million Jews who perished had been a refuge from life
for her, a schizoid retreat from the outer world. Simultaneously,
she had also used the Holocaust to gratify her oedipal strivings,
and as a defence against them. She could now see the extent to
which the Holocaust served as the link to her father, the only way
that she could become intimately close to him. She became aware
that by living in her father's past, as if she were with him before
her own birth, she was excluding her mother and siblings from
the dyad she had created. In the transference, she tried to exclude
me by expressing doubts regarding my expertise on the subject
of the Holocaust. Rachel now realised that since it was legitimate
to mourn the world of those who had perished, the Holocaust
had served as a disguise for her own longings for her father.
Becoming conscious of the double function which the Holocaust
served for her, and working through its defensive aspects, Rachel
took an important step towards separation from her father and
his traumatic past. 'My whole childhood was affected by a past
not my own', said Rachel, 'I took it upon me, I was living in a
world which wasn't this world.'

Elaborating upon her encounter with death allowed her to
rework the feelings of mourning and guilt evoked by the trauma.
Since her relationship with her boyfriend had been very private,
she felt unable to express her mourning as openly as she would
have liked. Being neither wife nor kin, she had no social outlet
for sharing her grief or receiving consolation. During this period,
she felt that it was only in analysis that she had the right to mourn.
She returned again and again to the night of the trauma, working
through her feelings of loss and guilt, trying to conquer them.

Rachel now viewed her mourning for victims of the Holocaust
in a different light. 'Look how we've distorted things! Instead of
seeing what we can learn from European Jewry, we're mourning
them all the time. It's like they died so that we could be traumatised and mourn them.'

Her conflict now consisted of a constant struggle between her
own self-destructiveness and her reparative impulses. The gradual
resolution of her depressive anxiety was achieved through a series
of reparative acts. Rachel strove to change her 'multiple identification with different languages and flags' (Rosenfeld, 1986) by
acquiring a new identity and becoming an Israeli citizen. Always
on the verge of leaving her place of work and profession, she
decided to remain in her field and found a respectable position.
Although her new job was in another city, she decided to continue

living in the same area and commute to work, in order to be close by for analysis. She tried to create a home for herself and purchased and furnished a nice flat. The flat, which symbolised her new self, was comfortable, tastefully decorated and filled with plants. It was very different from her cramped, untidy flat in the US.

Rachel now described herself as 'not disconnected anymore. I feel connected. Now, talking here about my present, I am in the present. Perhaps I could try to run away from the present, connect it to my father's past, but it doesn't work anymore ...'

With regard to object relationships, Rachel began a search for love and satisfaction in her own life. Compared to the way she had perceived herself before the trauma, as a replacement for her father's first son, she now felt more feminine. There was also a change in the way she perceived herself in her relationship to me, since her ego had become less split. 'I don't feel I am only an unconscious for you or a second generation symbol. You treat me like a person.' She felt that analysis, as well as the love she had received from her deceased boyfriend, made her aware of her real needs. She still expressed infantile wishes for love and protection, but also wanted to bestow her love on someone and, in the transference, on me. In spite of her frequently-appearing anxiety regarding the possibility that I might also suddenly disappear from her life, she now felt that the only thing which had real meaning for her was our deep, emotional relationship. After affirming the life-forces inside herself, Rachel again became involved in a relationship. This relationship (with a male colleague who knew her former boyfriend), despite its problems, helped her overcome her fears of being emotionally as well as physically destructive towards those she loved.

The birth of a separate self

Rachel's progress facilitated further analytic work, the purpose of which was separation from her mother. This phase lasted for about two years.

Rachel's ambivalent attitude towards her new boyfriend, as well as her corresponding relationship with me in the transference, indicated that despite her achievements in the previous phase, separation from her mother had not yet occurred. Rachel refused to marry her boyfriend, who offered her the opportunity of building a family together. She was unable to make a mature commitment to him. She saw him as a controlling, manipulative figure and claimed that, like her former boyfriend, he didn't

meet her family's standards (that is, her mother's expectations
of a future son-in-law). Rachel felt that rebuilding her life could
be done only at the expense of her mother's well-being, as if
separation would result in leaving a dead mother behind. In
this regard, Rachel brought up memories from her late adolescence and young adulthood of her mother's violent reactions to
her going out with men (being upset and sick in bed for days),
which caused her to avoid dating for many years. Rachel learned
to hide her private life from her mother and from the world, never
committing herself publicly to a relationship in order to avoid
her mother's wrath.

In the transference, as well as in her relationship with her
boyfriend, Rachel was searching for the care, control and manipu-
lation which she had experienced with her mother.

In analysis, we attempted to work through Rachel's conflicting wishes and expectations of me. On the one hand, Rachel longed
for the fulfilment of her infantile needs, attributing to me the role
of the pre-oedipal mother; on the other hand, she tried to transform
me into the phallic, controlling mother whom she hated, by
pressuring me to make decisions for her and to take responsibility for her life. My refusal to assume these roles was interpreted
by her as indifference and lack of caring. I helped Rachel realise
that if I fulfilled her wishes, it would curtail her freedom and
eventually destroy our relationship.

A difficult period in analysis ensued. Rachel attempted to run
away from her ambivalence towards me by ruminating obsessively
about her dilemma. She vacillated between marrying her boyfriend
and separating from him. Since I refused to make decisions for
her, she felt angry and frustrated. Afraid that her aggressive wishes
towards me might destroy me, she did not allow herself to express
them openly. Instead, she acted them out through the following
episode: Rachel skipped her regular session without notifying
me, and instead travelled to see a rabbi who was supposed to
provide her with the solution to her problem. Through this act
Rachel attempted to show me how ineffectual and useless I was
to her.

During this phase of analysis I occasionally felt hopeless. I was
no longer certain that my conclusions about Rachel's ability to
grow, based on the previous phase of analysis, were correct.
Moreover, I began to have doubts about my role as analyst in a
treatment which now appeared endless and barren. Gradually, I
became aware that these doubts stemmed from the fact that

Rachel had directed powerful aggressive tendencies of an unconscious nature against me, which nearly destroyed my faith in myself
and in the future of our work together. In the transference, a
complex elaboration of her hostile wishes towards me ensued. We
understood that her previous behaviour of clinging to me in
analysis was a way of making sure that I still existed, in spite of
her wish to destroy me. Her rejection of me (by ignoring transferential interpretations) stemmed from her fear of losing herself
in the relationship. As a result of the working-through process,
Rachel realised that I could contain her aggression without being
destroyed (losing hope); moreover, she experienced a feeling of
togetherness in analysis, which not only did not hinder but, on
the contrary, helped her grow as an individual.

Working through her hostile wishes towards me in the transference led Rachel to discover and elaborate upon her complex
relationship with her internal maternal object. Her emotional
experience with me in the transference helped her relinquish the
magical, omnipotent thought that by building a life of her own
she would destroy her mother. She began to believe that separation
need not be a violent, angry break. In the transference, she experienced me as capable of letting go of her and surviving, and
she even began to feel that her maturing was a source of satisfaction to me. As a result of her experience with me, Rachel, still
fearful, expressed the wish of giving up her life in hiding and of
building a family of her own.

Using me as an ally in her fight for separation, Rachel decided
to confront her parents with a request for their consent to her
marriage. A short but violent struggle ensued, in which the mother
again appeared adamant not to let go of her daughter. This time
Rachel's reaction was different. She did not fall to pieces under the
burden of the accusations, guilt and aggression which were heaped
upon her. Instead, she realised that her mother's difficulty in
separating from her did not have to hinder her from asserting her
own wishes. Both parents ultimately gave the couple their blessing.

Rachel's struggle with herself and her parents was crowned by
success. Rachel's marriage took place during her fourth year in
analysis with me, and she later became pregnant. In contrast to
her long struggle to become capable of living with someone, her
wish for motherhood was free of conflict. During this period we
were able to work through her anxiety regarding the delivery, as
well as the joy accompanying it. Moreover, Rachel's pregnancy
enabled us to re-examine several themes which we had dealt

with at the beginning of analysis: first, her search for the ideal mother, her father's former wife. Rachel raised this subject by way of a story about a friend of hers who couldn't conceive and adopted the baby of Ethiopian immigrants. Rachel believed that when this baby reaches adulthood, he will return to his own community to search for his real mother. We connected this to the fact that Rachel, who always felt that she was the black sheep of the family, came to Israel for the same purpose. Rachel felt that she had come a long way since then. Through her experience in analysis, she was able to work through her idealisation of her father's first wife as well as her anger towards her mother. Rachel now feels much closer, emotionally, to her mother; she invited her to stay with her after the delivery and is looking forward to her help and support.

The subject of naming the baby also connected us to the past. Rachel was wavering between naming the child after her father's dead son and using a modern Hebrew name. She decided on a compromise, out of respect for the past. The dead child's name would be used as a middle name. 'In everyday life, the child will be called by his first name', said Rachel. 'It is time to put an end to the story.'

During the past year, content with her marriage and with life, Rachel raised the question of terminating analysis. Looking back, she evaluated her process of growth: 'By getting married I kind of decided to become normal. I could very easily have spent my life without a family. I could have not married. I could have not become pregnant. I'm lucky to have my husband with me in the delivery room.'

Rachel recently informed me that she had found a trustworthy midwife to handle her delivery. In the transference, we understood that I am the midwife who helped her give birth to her own self.

I agreed to Rachel's request to terminate analysis. Over the remaining few months we dealt with her fears in this regard, as well as with her wish for independence. Like Rachel, I felt good that her 'interminable' analysis was finally coming to an end.

Discussion

I would now like to explore the following themes: (a) Rachel's need for concretisation; (b) the impact of re-traumatisation and working through it in analysis; and (c) the process of differentiation and growth which resulted from the analytic experience.

(a) In the first part of analysis, we attempted to search for Rachel's self through the revelation of family secrets (Gampel, 1982). We worked through the special bond that existed between Rachel and her father which made her re-create his past in her own life. This special bond made Rachel feel that she had shared her father's secret without having really known it, as if she had always been with him prior to her own birth (Klein, 1973a). Traces of this knowledge were probably transmitted to her through stories she might have forgotten, or even without words. After discovering her father's secret, Rachel felt the need to express her conflicts and her fantasies in this regard by externalising the past. She re-created her father's drama in a concrete way, playing different roles and assigning complementary ones to me in the transference. The concretisation of her wishes at the beginning of analysis reflected her confusion of self and object, past and present, fantasy and reality (Bergmann, 1982).

(b) Rachel's encounter with death allowed a reactivation and reworking of her sado-masochistic fantasies in relation to her father's first family. As a result of the actual trauma, she experienced mourning and guilt in a personal way. The quasi-mourning for the masses who perished (called 'transposition' by Kestenberg [1982, 1989]) changed into real mourning; her 'persecutory guilt' changed into 'depressive guilt' (Grinberg, 1964).

My interpretation of the tragic event, which showed Rachel the other polarity of hate, namely, love – was based on the link which Freud drew between these feelings and life- and death-forces. Freud stated: 'We started out from the great opposition between the life and the death instincts. Now-object love presents us with a second example of a similar polarity – that between love (or affection) and hate (or aggressiveness). If only we could succeed in relating these two polarities to each other and deriving one from the other' (Freud, 1920).

Rachel used my interpretation to absolve herself from the imagined crime of murder, because it helped her 'undo the fit between the actual trauma and early narcissistic fantasies' (Moses, 1978). The impact of re-traumatisation of persons suffering from trauma transmitted by their parents has been dealt with in greater depth in my paper 'Working through the vicissitudes of trauma in the analysis of Holocaust survivors' offspring' (Kogan, 1989a). *(c)* In the last phase of analysis, Rachel achieved greater maturity and growth by working through the separation from her mother. In the transference relationship, as well as in life, Rachel was in a state of chronic dilemma which preceded her oedipal development.

Rachel had an 'In and Out' relationship with me (Guntrip, 1980), in which she risked the loss of both me and herself. This was due to the fact that she had not yet outgrown the particular kind of dependence on love-objects that is characteristic of infancy. She was afraid of either being swallowed up in the relationship and thus losing her own individuality, or of destroying me by absorbing me into herself. Her needs were expressed through her powerful demand that I take care of her body (by ascertaining that she was eating, sleeping, defecating), which she tended to neglect when feeling rejected or upset. Like an infant, she felt that her needs were extremely urgent and vital, and if not quickly met, panic and rage developed. This 'need-relationship' (Winnicott, 1964) towards me in the transference had a dangerously intense, destructive aspect. This became clear to me from my feelings of helplessness and my doubts regarding my analytic role during this phase. Rachel attempted to destroy me in my capacity as analyst for not fulfilling her infantile needs. A struggle with her regressive urge to remain fused with me for the sake of comfort and security ensured. Through her unconscious, aggressive attack, Rachel strove to differentiate herself from me and find her own self. The analytic experience of me surviving her aggression without being destroyed (Winnicott, 1971) enabled her to separate from and deal with her ambivalence towards me.

At the same time, the object representation of her mother as a cold, intrusive woman who attempted to dominate her through anal struggles changed, her mother thus seeming less omnipotent and less threatening for her. As a result of this, Rachel felt less guilty and became less destructive towards herself. The process which took place in the transference recapitulated the entire process of developing a normal mixture of dependence and independence, characteristic of the mature adult.

I would like to conclude with Winnicott's statement about the terminability of analysis: 'There are many patients who need us to be able to give them a capacity to use us. This for them is the analytic task ... A backcloth of unconscious destruction of the analyst is set up, and we survive it, or, alternatively, there is yet another analysis interminable' (Winnicott, 1971). Rachel's analysis, an almost life-long process, was finally coming to an end.

III The Second Skin[4]

This chapter explores the relationship between self, body and object, as illustrated by the analysis of a Holocaust survivor's daughter. In treatment, the patient initially revealed her shattered self and her need for an emotionally containing object by means of bodily sensations. Her attempt, somewhat later, to communicate through drawings was midway between the pre-verbal language of the body and the verbalisation of a child. This phase paved the way for the reconstruction of the self in analysis, through verbal means of communication.

In this case illustration, the patient perceived the analytic experience as a 'second skin' – an emotional container which was capable of holding together different aspects of her personality.

Introduction

The link between body and self was established by Freud (1923), who defined the ego as 'first and foremost a bodily ego, not merely a surface but itself a projection of a surface'. By this, Freud underlined one of the most important factors which form the basis of one's identity.

Hoffer (1950) claimed that the distinction between self and not-self stems from the way one experiences one's body and what subsequently becomes environment; this is based on two sensations of the same quality elicited by the hand of the infant touching his own body. This factor contributes to the process of structural differentiation.

Mahler (1975) stressed the growth of the ego as first function-ing in the matrix of the narcissistic relationship, and later in the object-relationship to mother. When a child's capacity to use the mother 'as a beacon of orientation in the world of reality' (Mahler, 1968) is deficient, the ego apparatus, which usually grows in the matrix of the 'ordinary devoted' mothering relationship (Winnicott, 1962), fails to thrive; or in Glover's terms (1956a) the ego nuclei do not integrate, but fall apart.

Bick (1968) shed light on this idea from a different angle. In her opinion, the body's skin functions as a boundary which has an internal meaning: it holds together the different parts of the personality which, in their most primitive form, do not appear to have a force which binds them. This internal function of containing the parts of the self is dependent, initially, on the intro-jection of an external object, which is experienced as capable of fulfilling this function. Children who have no opportunity of iden-tifying with a containing object suffer from defective self-integration and from impaired differentiation between internal and external spaces.

Anzieu (1985), in his book Le Moi-Peau, as well as Houzel (1987) in the collection of essays of Anzieu and his team, Psychic Envelopes, elaborated upon Freud's idea of the ego as a structure charged with a precise psychic function; that is, to contain psychic excitation and block the free flow of quantities of excitation inside the mind (Freud, 1895). The ego is the surface which draws the line of demarcation between the individual's internal and external world, between the internal psychic world and the psychic world of other people, a surface to which Anzieu and Houzel refer as a 'psychic envelope'.

Pines (1980) stressed the fundamental importance of the skin to the development of the self. Pines viewed the skin as a means of communication between mother and infant, with the mother providing the holding environment. This is how primary iden-tification of the self is established.

In the following case illustration, both introjects are inadequate objects. The traumatised parent, in his own frantic search for an object which he can experience as something which joins together the disparate parts of his own personality, turned the child into a container. Thus, instead of fulfilling the role of an internal protective skin, the parent erected a permeable membrane between himself and the child through which he could not contain within himself.

Analysis revealed the patient's fragmented self resulting from the lack of a containing object, and the transferring of the symbolic representation of the object to the patient's own body (Szasz, 1957).

Case Illustration

Referral and evaluation

Kay, a twenty-six-year-old woman, married for seven years and the mother of two daughters (at the time aged two and five), was referred to me by a family friend who asked for an emergency consultation out of fear that Kay was going to realise her threats of suicide.

I ushered into my waiting room a large, fair-skinned woman in her forties, behind whom a girl who looked like a young adolescent was hiding. The girl's appearance was strange; she was small, thin, underdeveloped and her face was covered with acne.

The woman explained that she had made the appointment for Kay and would like to wait for her until the end of the session. Emerging from behind the woman, the girl curtsied, asked for a glass of water, dashed to the toilet, then walked towards my office, peeping into the other rooms along the way.

This first meeting revolved around Kay's feelings regarding the futility of her life, her wish to end it and her lack of courage to do so. She had recently begun climbing to the top of tall buildings, playing with the idea of throwing herself from them, but too afraid to act out her impulse. While telling me the story of her life, Kay snatched several pens from my desk and began playing a curious game of furiously taking my pens apart and slowly putting them back together. By watching her reconstruct a whole from the scattered pieces, I understood the message she was conveying to me through her game – her desire that I should reassemble the fragments of her own shattered self and bind them together by means of a life-giving force.

Kay was born in the US and emigrated to Israel several years ago. She had a high school and college education, but never succeeded in holding down a job. She regarded her coming to Israel and living with her husband's family as 'getting out from the gutter'.

Since the age of sixteen Kay lived away from home, changing places and jobs; she became promiscuous, experimented with drugs and was barely able to support herself.

In spite of having a nice husband and two delightful children, Kay felt that her life was a prison. She attempted to escape from it – sometimes by running away from home, at other times by attempting suicide.

Kay had several short encounters with psychiatric help: at the age of thirteen, after swallowing a large quantity of pills in order to 'get high'; at the age of sixteen, after an experience of 'almost rape' at a therapy centre for rape victims; and at the age of nineteen, after an automobile accident. In spite of a generally derogatory attitude towards psychiatry, Kay found her few therapeutic encounters very helpful.

I was very much aware of Kay's need for immediate, intensive help, and I recommended psychoanalytically oriented psychotherapy as the treatment of choice at this stage. Kay expressed her wish to discuss my suggestion with her husband; she wanted him to agree to pay for the treatment as she wasn't working and had no income of her own.

Several days later Kay phoned and asked me if I could see her together with her husband. I agreed and they arrived together. Her husband was a good-looking young man, robustly built and wearing military clothes, with the strange little girl hiding behind him. The young man appeared quite angry at what he called his wife's 'whims'. He thought that if she would make up her mind to be OK, then she wouldn't need any help at all. He himself did not believe in psychology and was doubtful about what I could do for her. He was a professional whose career was very important to him and he spent much time travelling abroad. He was very irritated by his wife's moodiness.

I realised that the young man felt threatened by the entire situation. I acknowledged how difficult it must have been for them to come for help. I emphasised my belief that Kay required help, adding that I would recommend her to a colleague who might be immediately available. The young man reacted by expressing his fears: his wife had made several attempts to jump from the eighth floor of the building in which they lived, and he was afraid to leave her alone when he travelled. He asked me to accept her for treatment, and even though it was difficult for him to finance payment he nevertheless planned to find a way.

I was struck by the parental way the husband spoke about his childlike wife. His outward attitude was that of a parent bringing his naughty child for therapy so that she would become disciplined and behave, although inwardly he was terrified by her threats of suicide.

Throughout this interview Kay sat very quietly, not uttering a single word.

Two days later, over the weekend, I received a phone call from Kay who did not seem concerned that she might be intrusive. She was bubbling over and bursting with joy. It seems that her husband had found a solution: he phoned 'Daddy' in the US and asked him to pay for the treatment. Obtaining her father's agreement, Kay's husband decided to keep half the money for the 'family' and use the remainder for therapy. Kay wanted to make an appointment with me as soon as possible in order to commence her treatment.

In my countertransference, I felt a heavy weight lying on my mind. Did I want to take upon myself the treatment of this childish, sick person who was already intruding upon my life in a very demanding way? Was I ready to bear the continuous tests which awaited me, especially her self-destructive tendencies? Could I face the possibility of failure in this case and had I not already been assigned the burden of fighting for her life?

That night I had a dream which confirmed just how frightened I was of the prospect of treating Kay. In my dream I saw Kay standing on a window-sill on the eighth floor, while I looked up at her from my office below. One of Kay's legs was dangling out of the window, she looked down at me, and attempted to jump, mocking my terror. I awoke with a start, aware of my fear but also feeling a commitment towards this woman. I was aware of the omnipotent wish she had evoked in me to catch her as she jumped. I felt that this would be a very difficult assignment, but she would make me feel guilty of murder if I were to leave her alone. Working through my countertransference feelings – the fear, the guilt and the saviour complex which she had evoked in me – I was aware of the heavy burden I was taking upon myself. In spite of all this, or perhaps because of it, I decided to accept Kay. I informed her that we would commence treatment the following week.

Case History

Kay is the oldest child in a complicated family set-up consisting of a mother, a stepfather, a brother one-and-a-half years younger and a stepsister her own age.

Both Kay's parents had very traumatic histories. Until the age of eight Kay's mother had lived in an institution for abandoned children in an environment of physical and psychological deprivation. At eight years old, she was adopted by a Baptist couple who provided her with care and affection. She married at the age of eighteen, and at nineteen gave birth to Kay. Kay's mother had a very difficult delivery and was considered clinically dead at the birth. The baby suffered from a severe disturbance during her feeding period because of an open oesophagus, and vomited most of the food she was taking in. After the birth of the second child, a boy, one-and-a-half years later, Kay's mother was advised not to have any more children, since childbirth endangered her life.

Kay was about two-and-a-half years old when her father abandoned his wife and children. After this event, her mother, lonely and depressed, began a frantic search for her origins. She discovered that her real father had been Jewish, and she decided to convert to Judaism. Shortly afterwards she met a Jewish man, eighteen years her senior, and married him. He became a father to Kay and she became very attached to him. Kay's stepfather was the sole surviving member of his family. His parents, sisters, brother and cousins had perished in concentration camps during the Holocaust. Moreover, when he was in Auschwitz, he underwent a Mengeles' experiment – castration by German doctors. He came to this marriage as a widower, bringing along his three-year-old adopted daughter who was the same age as Kay.

Kay's stepfather insisted on raising his children according to Jewish tradition, and they grew up in a Jewish atmosphere, aware of their Jewish identity.

Phase I – The shattered self behind the wounded skin

In treatment, the first issue we dealt with concerned Kay's death wishes and threats of suicide. She viewed suicide as a solution to her problems, and her belief in an afterlife made this alternative even more attractive.

In the initial therapeutic agreement, I warned Kay against acting upon this impulse, explaining to her that by destroying herself she would be destroying our therapeutic alliance. Only much later in treatment was Kay able to verbalise her feelings about this agreement, which was what gave her the strength and courage to go on.

In the first phase of therapy, Kay used non-verbal forms of communication, expressing herself mainly through bodily sensations and symbolic actions. For example, her wish to fall from high places was the concretisation of her feeling of 'falling apart' emotionally, which she could not yet verbalise. As a reaction formation to her wish to destroy herself, she exhibited an increased interest in her bodily sensations: her physical fitness, the strength of her muscles, her weight, and so on. In the transference, Kay often confused her feelings, not knowing if they belonged to her or to me, in a fusion process where differentiation was not fully possible.

The cruel, murderous side of Kay's personality was displayed without inhibition, unaccompanied by feelings of guilt or shame. Kay revelled in fantasies of bringing death to her husband and children, thus freeing herself of the responsibilities of married life and motherhood. In her dreams, she ran away from murderous figures who were trying to persecute her physically. In the transference relationship, I became the persecutor.

I will illustrate this theme with a series of dreams from this period.

> I dreamt about this young woman who attempted to kill me. She even tried to push my head in front of a car which was coming towards me. I tried to tell people that she wanted to kill everybody, but they didn't believe me. I know that I was right.

Kay's associations here revolved around the first time that she ran away from home. This occurred when her older daughter was about two-and-a-half years old. She ran away at night and stood in front of a truck, hoping to be run over by it.

In the transference, Kay felt that I was the one who was pushing her 'head' towards self-understanding, which could break her fragile defences. On a different level, we both understood that she was projecting her self-destructive aspect upon me, from which she also wanted me to save her.

Enquiring about the timing of this suicide attempt, we were able to link the distress that she felt at the time that her older daughter was two-and-a-half years old to the fact that her biological father had abandoned the family when she was of the same age. For the first time, Kay became aware of the possibility that she had been experiencing her father's abandonment as a wound which had been accompanying her throughout her life.

The theme of being at the mercy of a ruthless killer was repeated in the following dream:

In my dream there was a mass-murderer. He was cutting
people up into little pieces with a knife. The city had a very
sophisticated plan for catching him. I came home frightened,
locked the door, only to discover him sitting at my table.
Naturally, I was frightened. I tried to use the phone, but it
had been disconnected. He pointed a gun at my head and
no one could save me.

Kay's associations regarding the dream revolved around her
stepfather's story of woe, especially his castration by the Nazis.
Kay felt that, as a result of this terrible deed, all of his potential
children had been murdered. On the other hand, Kay saw her
stepfather as the persecutor. She described him as 'breaking people
down and then moulding them according to his wishes'.

In the transference, Kay was frightened of the power and
omnipotence that she attributed to me. As in the dream described
above, her aggressive, destructive aspect was projected onto me
and she had no hope of being saved from it. Working through
the transference relationship, Kay achieved some affective understanding: 'I think I am running away from the killer that is there
inside me', she said. 'I am my own worst enemy.'

Only later on would we be able to begin working through her
infantile wish to be my persecutor and destroy me, in order to
free herself from her infantile longings to be cared for.

Kay was like a forlorn, hungry child, longing for the breast while
at the same time rejecting it. She had noticeable anorexic traits;
her preoccupation with food playing a central role in her life. She
loved to eat, especially sweets; she controlled her craving for
food by fasting for entire days. She was always going around
hungry, especially when she came to our sessions, where she
would revel in fantasies about the tasty food she was going to have
when the session was over. Kay came to the sessions to be fed emotionally but, since she often furiously rejected the food I offered
her (that is, my interpretations of her longings) she would
frequently leave hungry.

Kay expressed her infantile need to be fed and taken care of
through symbolic actions: she would buy groceries at a store near
my office, in spite of the fact that she lived in another city; she
would arrive at the sessions with a bag full of vegetables; at
another time her bag would contain a bottle of milk and a diaper
intended to be used for her two-year-old child.

Kay suffered from the sensation of cold more than other people. She had recurrent dreams in which she searched for suitably warm clothing and shoes, which she was unable to find. This evoked tremendous anxiety in her, which she was unable to control. The anxiety she felt at those moments resembled that of a few-weeks-old infant, who becomes restless and upset when left unclad and feels threatened with disintegration; Kay's anxiety stemmed from her unconscious fantasy of endlessly falling, as if she were pouring out of herself (Grinberg and Grinberg, 1974).

Kay experienced me as a seamstress who sews new, better fitting clothing for her, which represented the outer 'skin' that she needed in order to feel whole and alive.

Kay's fantasy of overflowing and flooding me emotionally was expressed in the transference through another bodily sensation – weak bladder control. During her sessions, she would complain about her frequent need to urinate, and run to the toilet whenever she got very angry or excited. In this situation, Kay needed to see me as representing an external muscle, stronger than her own, which was capable of containing the emotions pouring out of her, without anger or retaliation.

Kay externalised her damaged container through her bad complexion. At the beginning of analysis, her face resembled a bleeding sore. Kay hated her face and avoided looking at herself in the mirror. We made the connection between the pimples on her face, which were visible to everyone, and the wounds which were in a secret place in her body, such as the vagina, in the form of herpes which she had contracted when young. The sores on her face, as well as those on her genitalia, made her feel defective as a woman.

In analysis I held a benign, accepting mirror to Kay, which gave her the opportunity to internalise a less impaired self-image.

The first change occurred when Kay felt secure enough to give up communicating primarily through bodily sensations, and tried another, still non-verbal mode. She began making small drawings during the sessions, which were accompanied by statements written in capital letters, intended to convey their respective meanings. The drawings, as well as the handwriting, had a very childish quality and the words were often spelled incorrectly, as if written by a young child. Among her drawings, there were pictures of boxes containing one word: for example, 'hate', 'hurt', 'anger'. One drawing, conveying a cry for help, depicted a helpless-looking child, under which was written: 'I

cannot do it any more. Summon the babysitter to save the child.'
A recurrent picture was of childish, simple loops surrounding a
man with a wiry flower emerging from his head, bearing the title
'Electricity'. The meaning of this drawing, which was related to
her fear of as well as her attraction to death, became clearer in
later stages of analysis.

I will now describe several drawings which conveyed Kay's
feeling of having an inner defective emotional container and her
wish for reparation.

One drawing was of an open treasure-chest containing a broken
record. Referring to this picture she explained: 'In the treasure-
chest there is me. I am made of three parts: them, me and the
part of me which was destroyed by them.' Another drawing was
of a box of toys with a missing lid. Underneath she wrote: 'I am
a box of toys. I want somebody to add part of me to me.' A third
drawing was of a fish in water swimming towards two words: 'Food';
'Love'. Alongside was her message: 'Make me whole.'

Kay asked me to collect her drawings and fasten them together
in a notebook, which she referred to as 'my book'. Doing this for
her, I realised that she was asking me to assemble the dispersed
elements of her shattered personality and bind them together with
a life-giving force.

Phase II – Reconstruction of the self

The previous phase, in which Kay felt sufficiently well-understood
and supported to first bring the fear-ridden infant, and subsequently
the unhappy child, into the relationship, paved the way for
analysis. This phase was necessary for building a feeling of safety
and trust from which verbalisation could emerge (Levine, 1985).
Kay proved herself capable of a good working alliance, and reached
the stage where she was ready to verbalise her memories ('I don't
need to draw anymore, now I can talk to you'). I suggested that
treatment continue in the form of analysis, which she readily
accepted.

In this phase of analysis, we dealt with the reconstruction of
the self along two main paths: (a) the reconstruction of Kay's
childhood; and (b) the working through of Kay's relationships with
internal object representations, leading to differentiation between
the self and the damaged introjects.

Kay experienced her mother as the first defective emotional
container in her life. Her feeling of almost being 'dropped' by her
mother before her birth was expressed through a recollection of

her mother's story about wanting to abort Kay when she was five months pregnant. The doctor convinced her mother of the hazards involved in such a procedure and she continued with the pregnancy.

In the transference relationship, Kay assigned to me the role of a doctor who has to save her from her own destructive tendencies, thus helping her to be born anew.

I will now describe how Kay perceived herself in light of the narcissistic injury inflicted by her mother's story, with an excerpt from analysis in which she described her journey to treatment that morning:

> I want to tell you about my journey to you today. In the morning I did my jogging and then I saw a cat that had just been run over, full of blood, its entrails coming out. I think that the cat had been pregnant, but the unborn kitten had also been squashed. You could see its open womb and the dead kitten inside. It's probably rotting already. Afterwards, I saw the little retarded girl who always goes past my house. She's a big girl now, a woman actually, but always behaves like a little child. Further on, I saw an old, crazy woman who was talking to herself all the time. In the end, when I arrived at your house, I got out of the car and saw a woman in a wheelchair. Her husband took her out of the wheelchair and transferred her to a car.

This excerpt showed aspects of Kay which expressed her hopelessness. Kay identified with the cat that was run over and even more so with the kitten that was squashed inside its mother's womb.

Another side of Kay was that of the mature woman who behaved like a child, which was why she saw her own reflection in the defective woman-girl who passed her on the street. Immediately afterwards she met her old, hopeless aspect, which was reflected in the crazy old woman who talked to herself.

Outside my house she saw a couple. Now we became the two of us. Kay assigned me the role of the partner who transferred his crippled wife (herself) from the wheelchair to the car, which symbolised the means for going on a long journey in analysis. Kay was going to travel, in spite of feeling so impaired.

Kay's recurrent dreams about aborting a baby or dropping one from her lap indicated her constant fear that, like her mother when pregnant, and her real father, I too might abandon her. Abandonment was experienced by her as a life-endangering blow, both physically and psychologically. Kay protected herself from this possibility. 'I am not dependent on you. One day you won't be here, I won't feel the loss, I won't fall apart.'

We were now able to work through Kay's dreams of persecution at the hands of murderers in light of her complex, painful relationship with her mother. I will illustrate this with the following dream:

> I was a person [Kay often addressed herself in this way, meaning that she felt she was neither man nor woman], and there was a man who forced me to promise him that I would kill myself – I don't remember why. He wanted me to cut a vein in my body. I couldn't do it. He did it for me. He wanted to leave me there with him until I died. I refused to die, I have not died.

Kay's associations revolved around the fact that on the previous day she had been babysitting at a friend's house while the friend went for a session with her psychologist. In response to my enquiry, Kay said that the friend was the lady who had brought her to me 'by the hand' for treatment. In the transference, we understood that I was the babysitter who had to protect the baby aspect inside her from her internal 'murderess mother'. At the same time, I was also the analyst-mother who might wound her and force her to stay with me forever, until death. The dream showed that, in spite of feeling that she was in danger, Kay's wish to live had become stronger.

Birth and death were connected in Kay's life from the beginning. Her mother had had a very difficult delivery. She was considered clinically dead at Kay's birth, and was 'reborn' afterwards. Kay's own flirtation with death was an expression of her unconscious wish that death pave the way to rebirth.

Kay described herself as a fragile baby who had suffered from a severe disturbance during the feeding period. In her opinion, her mother saved her life by feeding her frequently. In the transference, we came to understand that her frequent analytic sessions were vital for her. We also realised how important it was for Kay to know that I am always here, ready to 'feed' her, in spite of her frequent rejections of me.

After delivering her second child, Kay's mother became sick and was abandoned by Kay's father. Kay had a memory from when she was two-and-a-half years old of her mother remaining in bed all day long, and of herself, hungry, trying to prepare toast; Kay burnt her hand in the process, thus damaging her 'skin'. This memory was reinforced by later recollections of her mother addicted to amphetamines, forgetting to eat, lying in bed for days, preoccupied with the occult. Ever since she was a child, Kay had switched roles with her mother, taking care of her as if she were her baby. She also adopted willingly her mother's role in the relationship with her stepfather, by taking care of him when he came home from work.

Working through the relationship with her own children, and the repetition compulsion which characterised her behaviour towards them (on several occasions, Kay tried to abandon them and often beat them cruelly), raised other aspects of her mother's personality. Kay perceived her mother as physically violent and emotionally inconsistent. Although she was sometimes very tender and loving, she could suddenly become bossy and cruel, 'tearing into you with a sharp knife'. Her mother used to bite her children, pull their hair and, when angry, hit them viciously with the telephone wire. It took Kay a long time in analysis before she could trust my emotional stability, often fearing that my acceptance of her might change into cruelty or rejection. During this phase, we were able to work through her rejection of my interpretations of her oral longings. Kay explained that she found my ideas, like her mother's, 'crazy; weird', although she experienced the tone of my voice as possessing the quality of milk. In the transference, I was the 'good breast' and at the same time the 'bad persecuting internal breast' (Klein, 1932).

In my feelings of countertransference, I often experienced Kay as an angry, biting infant who was trying to destroy my analytic prowess through her depression and lack of hope. This was illustrated by an episode from analysis. Kay had been feeling very depressed of late. She came to analysis stressing over and over that everything was useless. In this session, her thoughts revolved around the firstborn (who was born dead) of the friend who had brought her for treatment. 'Can you imagine?' said Kay, 'what it is like to bear a dead foetus inside your womb?'. In my countertransference, I felt hopeless and depressed. I knew that Kay was asking me about herself; she was the dead foetus in my womb. I also felt totally impotent, confronted with her demand to give her life. I then realised that by making me feel so helpless Kay had turned me into her own dead foetus, a foetus inside the womb of an angry woman who does not want to give birth to the live aspects of her self. Gathering my thoughts, I pointed out to Kay that she probably felt that she was a squelched, almost dead foetus in my womb, while at the same time she wanted to destroy the hope of being born alive. I continued by adding that lately I had felt she was testing my strength. I stressed that her underlying wish was that I shouldn't drown in her anger and depression so that she could be born out of my womb, a healthier, better integrated person. Kay sat in reflective silence for a while. Then I heard the relief in her voice as she said, 'You are so stubborn, even more than I am. That's good!'

Kay's mother had had a tremendous influence upon her life and identity. Kay felt that she was similar to her mother, identifying with her mother's childish, needy personality and lack of ability to deal with life.

Kay's internal representation of her stepfather emerged in analysis through a transferential experience: Kay became paralysed with fear if she arrived several minutes late to her session. She was afraid of my ensuing anger and retaliation. Working through this situation brought back terrifying memories of her stepfather. 'Father was a *Kapo*, he ran the house like a terror organisation', said Kay. She could never be late with her stepfather. She was terrified just by the look on his face. 'I wasn't a beaten child', continued Kay, 'I was battered psychologically.'

On the other hand, Kay described her special bond with her stepfather. She greatly admired his charm and enormous strength. She described herself as his favourite child, the only one who could talk to him. The others were too afraid to get close, including her mother, who behaved like one of the children. Kay's stepsister hated and resented her all through life for taking her place in her father's affections. When her stepfather came home from work, Kay would take off his shoes, bring him tea and chat with him. Her stepfather was also a nurturing figure: he was the person who prepared the meals at home. Kay related a dream in which her stepfather prepared a nice meal, avoiding using the oven. This little detail reminded her that, in reality, her stepfather had never used the oven but would always scare the children by threatening to cook them in the oven. We were able to connect this to Kay's recollections of her stepfather's story about his own mother and sisters who had been burnt in the ovens, while he had been selected as a *sonderkommando*, whose task it was to collect the bodies.

Kay reconstructed a home atmosphere in which feelings of fear and aggression prevailed. Her stepfather, whom she perceived as a good man at heart, used some cruel methods for imposing his will. Home often felt like a prison. The children's usual punishment was being 'grounded' – confined to home. To this day, Kay carries a feeling of curfew with her, and is unable to go very far away from home for more than a few hours at a time. For her, home, as well as the emotional home in analysis, was both a prison and, at the same time, a place of safety.

Kay didn't know many details of her stepfather's experiences during the war, because he kept them mostly to himself.

The atmosphere at home was one of silence, hiding a past full of terror and violence. Kay's stepfather had been writing his memoirs of the Holocaust for the last twenty years, but Kay never had the courage to ask to see them. In analysis, after working through her fear of discovering what had really happened to her stepfather, and encouraged by my supportive attitude, she decided the time had come to do so. To her great surprise and excitement her stepfather sent her his autobiography, which he dedicated to his children. Kay read it avidly, and brought it to me so that I could read it as well, thus making me a partner to 'the search for the self through family secrets' (Gampel, 1982). At long last the cry that had been hidden, the voice of the Holocaust, broke through! This enabled us to begin the exploration of the way Kay had communicated with me during the first part of treatment, which had been the way she had lived her life until then – using her body to express unconscious fantasies pertaining to the bodily sensations, anxieties and emotions experienced by her stepfather during the Holocaust. Traces of these experiences had been transmitted to her either narratively or mimetically, through acting out. Books and movies on the Holocaust had always had a personal meaning for her. For example, there was a film on this subject which she had seen in a college course, in which she imagined she saw her own father among the men, towels wrapped around them, awaiting castration by the Germans.

We could now understand Kay's constant preoccupation with her body, her physical fitness, her weight and her muscles, as part of her survival complex. It was based on her unconscious fantasy that 'I feel my body, therefore I exist.'

In the transference, we attempted to understand her preoccupation with her body on a more symbolic level. I will illustrate this with the following excerpt from analysis, which occurred at the end of a session (K = Kay; I = Ilany):

K: Yesterday I began a course in body-building. I went to lift weights. How was it? Wonderful. I did sixty push-ups; the man said that my stomach would ache but next time I'll do a hundred. I feel big, strong; it's fantastic. I did this and that (she lifts her hands up and down), I worked out for almost an hour. I focused on my hips and I'm in great shape now.

I kept quiet, feeling overcome by sadness even though Kay seemed so enthusiastic about her deeds. I realised then that I was identifying with her split-off sadness which she was projecting upon me. Kay continued:

K: You have to come with me to do body-building. In this place where we lift weights, I'm the only woman. I need more women there. We spend a quiet evening there lifting weights. It's fun, you know.
I: I think you're sharing your feelings about analysis with me now. Here we are lifting the burden of the past which is weighing upon your heart. It's difficult but also fun.
K: Yes, that's what it feels like today. Sometimes I feel indifferent. What is analysis for me? It's a place to go to, it's a place of hope. Not that I have a lot of hope, but ... I think that I will always remain the same, I don't think I'll ever change. Sometimes it seems hopeless.
I: I think that sometimes you want to destroy the hope I hold out to you; that hope is actually your own hope. Analysis is a place where we lift weights together, a place where you bring the hopeful and hopeless aspects of yourself.
K: (looking at her watch) What, do I have to go already? I'm totally confused today, I wish I could stay longer ...

In analysis, Kay had complained at length about her defective sense of smell. Only now could we make the connection to her stepfather's story about people dying in their excrement and vomit, not being able to 'make it' to the public latrine because of the awful stench emanating from it. Thus, impairment of the olfactory sense became a survival mechanism.

Kay's constant state of hunger, as well as her suffering from cold and her inability to find suitably warm clothing, were primarily part of her stepfather's experiences during the Second World War.

In connection with her fear of incontinence, Kay brought up a story of woe and humiliation from her stepfather's memoirs:

Father stood for hours on roll call, peeing in his pants, knowing that any movement could incur the death punishment. Urine was also the substance used by her stepfather to treat a wound on his leg, caused by the brutal kick of a German soldier. The wound took a long time to heal. During this phase of analysis, Kay felt that she was treating the wounds in her soul with bits of information from her repressed consciousness, things which she had known but forgotten over the years.

Kay's stepfather, the Nazi victim, physically mutilated and psychologically battered, became a Nazi hunter after the war, thus becoming the persecutor himself. Kay's dreams, in which she was the victim of a vicious killer, as well as the killer himself who wanted to murder everybody, illustrated her wish to identify with both these aspects of her stepfather.

We understood that her attraction to death by falling from high places was connected to her stepfather's 'Mythos of Survival', which consisted of the awareness of his conflictual emotions and unconscious wishes about living and dying (Klein, 1981; Klein and Kogan, 1986): he had survived death by standing naked an entire night in the cold, between the electric wires. Falling would have meant touching the wires and electrocution. During this period, Kay asked me for her book of drawings so that she might look through it. She found the drawing entitled 'Electricity', portraying a man with a wiry flower of death coming out of his head. The flower of death symbolised the electric wires which her stepfather had survived, but which had been inserted into Kay's head instead. 'Daddy put an electric prodder into me' said Kay. 'It is one with which you kill cows. Daddy is embedded in my own self.'

The mutilation resulting from her stepfather's castration was transmitted to Kay on both a physical and psychological level. The terrible fact was that her stepfather had volunteered for the operation, which was represented to him as a medical check-up together with the promise of a day off from work. The operation was performed twice, and each time a testicle was removed. After the first operation, he was able to mobilise his strength to recover. The second time, he experienced the finality of his castration as a deathly blow. He survived only because of the tactfulness and support of his fellow prisoners who helped him both physically and emotionally. As we have seen, Kay herself felt genderless: she referred to herself as a 'person' or 'neutral', her unconscious fantasy being that she, like her stepfather, was a castrated creature. This feeling was reinforced by the fact that Kay did not like to be touched or petted, and seldom achieved sexual satisfaction. Until she became pregnant, she had lived with the fantasy that she could never have children. On an emotional level, Kay considered herself incapable of giving and receiving love; she viewed her stepfather as her persecutor and accused him of this mutilation, at the same time identifying with his role of victim. 'Daddy castrated his children', said Kay. 'I was sterilised emotionally by him.'

I now want to focus on an aspect of the complex relationship between Kay and her stepfather, which is relevant to our subject; that is, the unconscious link to her stepfather's damaged body, which was perpetuated in her sexual relationship with her husband as well as upon her own body.

During treatment, we had the opportunity to work through Kay's relationship with her husband. He represented a parental figure for her, upon whom she felt as dependent as a baby, while at the same time hating him for it. She felt that she was his prisoner, the way she felt in her parents' home.

Kay became acquainted with her husband during one of his trips to the US, where he worked for some time. After a short while, they had sexual relations and she discovered that he was impotent most of the time. Through a lot of tenderness and patience she helped him overcome this difficulty. She still believed that this was the reason he married her.

We were now able to connect Kay's wish of repairing her husband's virility with her unconscious wish of repairing the damage which was inflicted upon her stepfather. It was only through the episode of concretisation, which I will describe below, that we were able to explore Kay's compelling need actually to carry out the reparation of her stepfather's castration upon her own body.

After my summer holiday, Kay came to her session and informed me that during my absence she had undergone breast surgery. She stressed the fact that she had chosen to do it when I was away because she did not want to cancel her sessions after I returned home. Elaborating on the subject, Kay explained to me that the operation was the fulfilment of a wish she had had since she was young – to enlarge her breasts with silicone implants. Kay paid a visit to a doctor who examined her breasts and informed her that they weren't small, but 'empty'. The doctor told her that an operation was possible but it was not without risks. She was also warned of the possibility that her body might reject the silicone, a fact which is accompanied by tissue inflammation, fever, pain, and further operations. She was told that she might never be able to breast-feed if she were to have another child. Despite being terrified by these prospects, Kay nevertheless decided to go ahead with the operation. She was referred to a shop where she was measured for the implants and selected them from a catalogue. She chose a medium size which she felt would make her look much more like a 'whole' woman.

Kay came to analysis on the appointed date, two weeks after the operation. She entered the room walking upright and, pulling her blouse against her breasts, asked if I could see any change. Only afterwards when lying on the couch did she tell me the story. She was joyful and stressed her satisfaction with her ability to conquer her fears.

In my feelings of countertransference, I felt a heavy weight burdening my heart. This made me aware that Kay was not in touch with her sadness, which was conveyed to me by massive projective identification.

Attempting to understand what had compelled her do this deed during my absence, I pointed out to Kay that she had only begun feeling that her breasts were 'empty' when I was not around, when she wasn't getting the feeding and support from our regular sessions. Kay laughed a short laugh and then confirmed my hypothesis in an angry voice: 'I don't need you; I don't need anybody. I want to depend only on myself.' I showed Kay that her need to 'fill' her breasts stemmed from her anger and frustration caused by her feeling that she had been abandoned by me. Gradually, Kay became aware of these feelings and accepted them.

Working through these feelings in the transference led Kay to reveal her fantasies of flirting with death on the operating table. She had undergone the operation in order to repair her femininity, but she also thought she might die because of it. Of course, she now felt that she had once again overcome a terrible danger.

Kay associated her victory over her possible death on the operating table with a story from her stepfather's life. After the war, her stepfather met one of the few men who had survived the castration procedure in the Mengeles experiments. The man told him about a Jewish doctor in Paris who performed surgery on these people – that is, implantation of testicles – free of charge. Her stepfather decided to go to Paris and have the operation. It was successful and he was able to resume sexual relations with women but remained infertile.

We now attempted to understand Kay's need to act out her stepfather's life story on her own body. I pointed out to Kay that she might have been trying to implant her femininity into her breasts, in the same way that her stepfather had had his manhood implanted into his 'empty' testicle sacs.

A pregnant silence filled the room as Kay absorbed my words. Then, understanding the meaning of her action, she was overwhelmed by a powerful surge of emotions. It took us a long time to work through her feelings of fear, depression and pain which replaced her euphoric demeanour. Furthermore, we now tried to elaborate on her complex needs which she expressed through her deed. Consciously, she was trying to attain a better, repaired sexuality. Unconsciously, she was attempting to endanger herself in a concrete way, to come as close as possible to an imagined death in order omnipotently to overcome it.

By repeatedly working through these painful, compelling motives Kay was able to form a link between her feelings and her thoughts, which until then had been severed by repression (Freud, 1915a). Working through her feelings following the lifting of the repression in the transference helped Kay reach some affective understanding of her actions, and eventually facilitated a better differentiation between herself and her internal paternal object.

Evaluation

The analytic process described here is too short for evaluating all of the changes which occurred in Kay's life. However, I will mention briefly some of them.

The process of working through Kay's relationship with representations of primary objects facilitated the differentiation between the stepfather's experiences and Kay's infantile fantasies of destruction and loss. The object representation of the stepfather as a murderer and a hero changed, and he thus became less threatening for Kay. As a result of this, she felt less guilty and less destructive towards herself. She also felt safe enough to express her feelings in a more verbal way, and her suicidal thoughts began to disappear. The process of individuation was not yet complete because Kay expressed it in the form of a wish: 'Daddy had an enormous influence on me. I filled my entire life with the Holocaust. That was his legacy. I want to be free of Daddy, to get rid of this inheritance.'

Kay's outward appearance changed considerably. The wounds on her face cleared up nicely, although her facial tissue will always be scarred. She felt more mature and her feelings regarding her femininity greatly improved. She was able to achieve much greater sexual satisfaction. In addition, her attitude towards her children changed. Not only did she no longer run away from home, but she now treated them with sensitivity and affection. The change in her relationship to external and internal objects was linked to a change in her relationship to her own self: 'I am not a crazy little girl any more. I didn't even notice that I grew up. Now I'm a woman. I grew up a lot in the last two years – twelve years in two years.'

Kay was able to express her feelings of gratitude, and also to accept the symbolic 'food' extended to her in analysis. 'When I was falling', Kay said, 'you caught me and fed me. You are now part of my life.'

Kay still had many problems to grapple with, such as her inability to function in the world outside her home, or to fill her life with a job or interests other than her family. She still felt the need to hold my hand while 'walking on the tightrope of life'. Her wounded self, like her bad complexion, was healing, but the scars might always remain.

In spite of her difficulties, Kay felt that it was now possible to live. It was clear to both of us that the analytic process would have to continue for a long period of time.

Discussion

I would like to explore the relationship between self, body and object as it is reflected in the patient's growing sense of separateness in the transference.

Forming an identity is a process that stems from the mutual and successful assimilation of all the fragmentary identifications of childhood (Grinberg and Grinberg, 1974), the ego gradually choosing those fragments it identifies with (Erikson, 1956).

It appears that while the patient consciously felt that she was identifying with her mother in the role of a needy, helpless child, the unconscious facets of her ego (Szasz, 1957) related to her body as if it were her traumatised stepfather. This phenomenon can be perceived in terms of a complete union with a marvellous yet atrocious inner object, obliterating the inner boundaries between the ego and the incorporated object (Milner, 1952).

By transferring the symbolic representation of the object to her body (Szasz, 1957), the patient made an attempt at mastery through concretisation (Bergmann, 1982). This phenomenon led to living in two separate realities. The unconscious part of the self that was linked to the stepfather's past played the role of a primitive super-ego image, while the other part, which was better adapted to reality, assumed the role of a submitting ego. Persecutory anxiety stemmed from this split.

The background to the patient's identification with her stepfather was her traumatic abandonment by both parents. Her real father abandoned the family when she was two-and-a-half years old, estranging himself for ever; her mother, sick and depressed, was unable to give her the 'good-enough mothering' (Winnicott, 1962) she required. Her stepfather entered her life at a moment of physical and emotional deprivation; he simultaneously filled the roles of father and mother, his adopted children providing a substitute for the children he could never have.

The patient's bodily identification with her stepfather was based on her unconscious, omnipotent fantasy of saving him. By constantly proving her ability to survive in the face of danger or deprivation, the patient omnipotently vanquished the death and castration which threatened him. This identification also helped her stepfather avoid mourning his lost family and manhood. This can therefore be considered a 'substitute-for-mourning' mechanism (Bergmann, 1982).

The process of separation from me in the transference was expressed in the progress in the patient's mode of communication. At the beginning of treatment, she expressed herself the way an infant does, through bodily sensations; needing me on a concrete level. There was a striking correspondence between her adult mode of functioning and the anxiety of an infant (Sandler, 1977). During this phase she felt a total fusion with me, not sure to whom the feeling she expressed belonged. Like the child in the primal state, she was unaware that boundaries exist and she discovered them through play (Milner, 1952). By drawing, she expressed her subjective imaginary world without confusing it with the real world. Like a child in play therapy, she revelled in an atmosphere where 'adult suggestions, mandates, rebukes, restraints, criticisms, disapprovals, support, intrusion don't exist. They are all replaced by complete acceptance and permissiveness to be herself' (Axline, 1969). This phase served as a 'refuelling dialogue' (Sandler, 1977), with the patient scanning the analyst and herself for sensory and affective cues which could provide her with a sense of security. This refuelling bolstered her feelings of self-sufficiency and autonomy, so that she was gradually able to separate from me and deal with her ambivalence and with the new experience of verbalisation without too great a threat to her inner sense of security. Verbalisation means the forming of symbols and is therefore a tool for achieving differentiation. Instead of trying to externalise an inner meaning through actions or sensations, we tried to understand and translate them into a cognitive mode. The patient became aware of the unconscious meaning of her actions, a fact which lead to a diminished need for acting out.

Along with the process of separation from me in analysis, we found the process of differentiation from primary object representations. The patient's quest for truth and her need to know about her stepfather's past was an attempt to mourn reality rather than illusory shadows (Kestenberg, 1982). By doing this, she was ready to give up her world of fantasised trauma, which had kept her ego fixated on the unknown – the missing piece of her stepfather's history. Thus, she used what had happened to her stepfather in reality to amend what her ego had done to itself in fantasy. In this way, she began to differentiate between her stepfather and her introjected representation; between his experiences and her own bodily sensations.

Her stepfather, as well as her mother, had been internalised as emotionally impaired containers. Both parents projected their own depressive, aggressive tendencies onto the child, thus using her as a self-object for decreasing the enormous amount of depression and self- destructiveness which might have been fatal to them (Klein and Kogan, 1986).

The gradual internalisation in analysis of a holding environment, and of the analyst's representation as an emotionally adequate container – a 'second skin' – which holds together different aspects of the personality, eventually led to a more mature, better integrated self.

IV A Journey to Pain[5]

> *'What the sufferer does not grasp is the difficult task of relating to suffering – there lies his real suffering – suffering within suffering.'*
>
> H. Michaux (1944)

This chapter explores the restoration of the capacity to feel pain and guilt through a description of the analysis of a woman whose four-month-old baby died in a car accident due to her reckless driving. Analysis revealed that this incident was the result of the patient's need to repeat and actualise her unconscious fantasies and conflicts connected to her parents' feelings of survival-guilt. In the transference, this need found expression in the patient's attempt to destroy the analyst by a series of attacks on the therapeutic relationship. The analyst's ability to survive these attacks without retaliation enabled the patient to differentiate between her self and the beloved objects and relinquish her omnipotent ideas regarding her own destructiveness.

The analytic experience facilitated the emergence of the patient's feelings of mourning and guilt, from which she had protected herself by erecting strong defences. This led to the revivification of her psychic life and the reintegration of her self.

Case Illustration

Josepha, a thirty-seven-year-old scientist, married and the mother of a two-year-old daughter, decided to seek psychoanalytic help because of her feelings of emptiness and the futility of living. She had long toyed with the idea of analysis, but had not been able to summon the courage to make a commitment to it.

Josepha is the protagonist in a very tragic story. At the age of thirty-one she was involved in a terrible car accident. Her baby, a four-month-old girl, was next to her on the front seat in an ordinary infant seat which was not secured with a safety harness when Josepha suddenly crossed the dividing line of the highway and collided with a car approaching from the opposite direction. The baby was killed; Josepha's legs and pelvis were broken, her teeth were largely destroyed and her jaw bone fractured. She lay unconscious for ten days and awoke in the hospital where she was informed of her daughter's death. Faced with the loss of her child, Josepha wished herself dead, but she survived none the less. She underwent a series of orthopaedic and dental operations, which she experienced as very traumatic. After spending some time in a wheelchair she returned to work, walking on crutches. Contrary to medical expectations, she eventually regained her ability to walk, and only a slight limp remained. She had dentures made and her jaw bones were repaired, although she had difficulty opening her mouth. Three years after the accident, Josepha gave birth to another daughter.

Josepha sought professional help at a period in her life when she felt she had already overcome the irreversible effects of the accident. At the same time, a feeling of psychic numbness, an inability to feel joy or pain, accompanied by a sense of futility and meaninglessness, made her decide to seek help.

I will now briefly describe my feelings when confronted with Josepha's catastrophe at our initial meeting. I must admit that I was disconcerted and somewhat frightened at the prospect of treating this woman. I wondered about what happens to the psyche of someone whose death-wishes are realised in so horrible a manner, due to her own destructive deeds. I wondered whether psychoanalysis could help someone who loses a child under such terrible circumstances and whose entire psychic life appeared to be paralysed.

Years ago I had read several newspaper accounts of Josepha's accident which were accompanied by pictures of her in the orthopaedic department of the hospital, wrapped in bandages, her legs in traction. The lurid headline was 'I killed my baby', and the accident was described in detail. I remember being shocked and revolted by the journalistic 'scoop'. It never occurred to me that, years later, Josepha would come to me for analysis. When she first appeared in my office, I thought she displayed a courage that I myself, under similar circumstances, might not have been able to demonstrate. But to clearly understand her experience of loss, to give her holding, I had to be accessible to her fear that she was responsible for the irrevocable loss of her child.

This became clearer to me when, in reaction to her account of the accident, I was unable to feel either fear or pity, but was overcome by a feeling of numbness. I gradually realised that I was protecting myself from the terror that was conveyed in her story, as well as identifying with the defences which enabled her to continue functioning in this world. I wondered whether my personal experience with suffering was sufficient to enable me to accompany her on her analytic journey. Was it desirable to awaken the pain of mourning and the burden of guilt, in order to revivify her psychic life, and if so, at what price? And if revivifying her psychic life was the aim of analysis, would this indeed be possible?

Case History

Josepha was the second daughter of a farming family. Her parents were close to forty when she was born. During her first year of life, her father was mobilised for over a year and her mother had to shoulder the heavy burden of running the farm alone.

Josepha's parents had arrived in Israel as teenagers, after finishing high school in Eastern Europe. Her mother had two older brothers and a sister whom she had never met, since the sister had emigrated to the US before Josepha's mother was born.

When Josepha's maternal grandfather died, her mother, who had had a Zionistic upbringing, was sent alone to Israel. She went to live on a kibbutz where she met her husband who came from a similar background. They decided to leave the kibbutz, bought land and built a farm, starting from scratch. They considered this project vital to their existence.

Josepha grew up with stories of famine and suffering caused by lack of food. Josepha knew almost nothing about her father's family. She only knew that he had been very attached to his own father – after whom she was named – who had died after her father had immigrated to Israel.

I shall now describe the different phases of analysis which are relevant to our subject. The first three phases took place over the course of about two years, and the last phase continued for another year and a half.

Phase I – The fragmented self behind the fractured jaw

During the first sessions, Josepha conveyed to me the sense of the terrible catastrophe that had befallen her through her fragmented, incoherent speech. Her jumble of ideas and words brought to my mind an image of debris scattered in all directions during a car accident. It gradually dawned upon me that her disconnected sentences were an example of her inability to hold her own fragmented personality together.

In the here-and-now of the analytic session I felt lost and disoriented, moving in a chaotic, meaningless world. I realised that this was Josepha's way of conveying to me her own feelings of confusion and loss. Moreover, I felt trapped in a sado-masochistic game in which I was assigned alternately the roles of victim and persecutor.

When she cast me as the victim, Josepha was attempting to drown me in her incomprehensible discourse, which left me feeling paralysed and numb. When I pointed out to her that I was sane and alive in demanding to understand her gibberish, she immediately assigned me the role of a persecutory object. My attempts to assemble her words and ideas into a more coherent pattern, to enable us to extract meaning from them, was experienced by her as oppressive. She rebelled against being 'pushed towards normality', and rejected meaning as belonging to another world 'where your language prevails'. She experienced coherence, intelligibility and integration as threats to her fragmented self, which she named 'a conglomeration of worlds'.

Josepha abhorred reality and viewed me as its representative. She played omnipotently with the reality of time by being late for our sessions, but always 'on time' on her own watch. 'Her' time was different from mine, different from the time which analysis forced her to accept. Josepha frequently twisted my interpretations, emptied them of meaning and rejected them. I became aware that an encounter with her fantasised murderous aspect was unavoidable.

Josepha's gibberish was usually accompanied by inadequate affects, such as a fixed smile and a joyful demeanor. I often felt bewildered and asked myself whether she wasn't psychotic. There were, however, two important areas which demonstrated that Josepha did have some ego resources: her ability to take care of her family and her ability to function in the scientific world.

Josepha was apparently capable of being more coherent when it was necessary for her to function in the world. However, she considered this a mask behind which she hid her real, fragmented self. Josepha warned me not to encourage her to fake normality during the sessions.

Her dreams were another area which seemed to be more 'connected', pointing to a healthier self. The dreams usually formed a clearer, more intelligible narrative, as if the primary and secondary processes – her unconscious and conscious thoughts – had exchanged places. I gradually concluded that Josepha longed to establish a special kind of relationship with me based on over-sensitive rapport: I was supposed to know how she felt and what she thought without her communicating to me in words. For her, this constituted the only intimate, valid and nourishing way of relating to objects.

In this phase of treatment, I formulated several working hypotheses:

(a) Josepha's speech-splitting symbolised the way she experienced her fragmented self (body and psyche).

(b) Josepha resented treatment which employed verbal thought for solving emotional problems (Bion, 1955). She feared and hated me for attempting a psychoanalytic understanding of her problems, partly because she felt that psychoanalysis demanded of her the very verbal way of thinking she so feared.

(c) Josepha's destructive attacks on our verbal intercourse during our sessions symbolised the way she had related to primary love objects throughout the course of her life. I assumed that this was all connected to an escape from feeling guilty; that is, she would rather be fragmented, infantile and psychotic than feel guilty of murder.

Phase II – The gateway to mental pain

During this phase of analysis we searched for Josepha's imprisoned feelings. By means of a dream, Josepha expressed her wish to gain strength from the therapeutic relationship and escape her inner prison. In the dream, Josepha found herself in the science department dressed in prisoner's clothing; she lost her way, felt totally disoriented, could not find the gate out. Across the road she saw sick people who were hospitalised in a psychiatric ward. She felt close to them in spite of the distance. She searched for help. A young woman approached her and interpreted her dream for her. 'Don't you see that I need to be taken by the hand and shown to the gate?' Josepha asked. The woman redoubled her efforts to help her. Josepha felt that her efforts were all in vain. Suddenly, she made a decision, followed the woman, and found the way out. It was a long journey.

In her associations regarding the dream, Josepha referred to her ambivalent feelings towards me. She viewed me as unable to help her and considered my interpretations to be useless. Only recently did she begin to have some faith in analysis.

Progress in the reintegration process, the gradual fusion of the multiple splits of her personality into fewer and fewer fragments which enabled her at long last to bring meaning into her sentences and understanding into treatment, occurred when Josepha became acquainted with her psychic pain. This pain was located on the map of her psyche, 'at the frontiers and juncture of body and psyche, of death and life' (Pontalis, 1981).

It was because psychic pain was strikingly so absent in Josepha that I realised that she was refusing to encounter what might overwhelm her. Emotionally, Josepha felt empty and dead; guilt and mourning were foreign to her repertoire of feelings. The physical counterpart of this was the numbness of her body, the total lack of physical pain from her terrible injuries. Josepha was proud of her ability to induce this numbness.

In analysis, the first change occurred when Josepha allowed herself to encounter pain through a toothache. This unassuageable pain was caused by pressure on a nerve; Josepha claimed that there were people who, faced with such pain, lost consciousness, took morphine, or committed suicide. She herself preferred to come to analysis instead. We both became aware of the enormous courage required of her for encountering an excruciating physical pain, which symbolised the revivification of her psychic pain. Josepha credited me with the power to alleviate the pain evoked by treatment, the very pain whose purpose was to save her from the inner death to which she had committed herself.

Just as she had delayed seeking analytic treatment, Josepha put off going to the dentist. When she finally did go to him, she projected her guilt upon him and claimed that he was so impressed by her suffering that he gave her a piece of chocolate before operating on her tooth, like granting the last wish of a person condemned to death. Josepha was afraid that I might feel pity for her out of guilt and my inability to withstand the pain which I was causing her, and thus lose objectivity. Thus, the analytic 'operation' which she had to undergo in order to revivify the dead part of her was simultaneously experienced by her as a terrifying execution, a threat to her existence because of the overwhelming feelings of pain and guilt which it revived in her.

In the transference, Josepha assigned me the role of the dentist who had to perform the extremely difficult task of treating her tooth through the impaired opening of her mouth. Work on the rotten tooth was meant to ease the pain caused by pressure on the nerve, but forcing the mouth open was in itself an agonising procedure. For Josepha, to 'open her mouth' in analysis – to put words and sentences together into a meaningful, coherent narrative – was immensely threatening, since it ushered in the awareness of psychic reality and with it the depression which is linked to the destruction and loss of good objects.

Josepha's associations with the bad smell emanating from the rotten tooth in her mouth brought us closer to her inner reality. The smell of decay reminded her of a foul smell in the entrance hall of her house. She was quite sure that there was a dead cat or dog in one of the closets, which should be opened so that the corpse could be discarded and the lobby freed of the stench. She was determined to find the 'corpse' inside herself, unaware that she herself might have been its executioner.

Phase III – The reconstruction of the trauma

Conquering her fear of searching into her past, Josepha began to relate some intelligible childhood memories which gave us an idea of the atmosphere in which she had grown up.

Josepha has two sisters, ten years and nine years older than herself, who are also scientists. The sisters were her mother's favourite children and Josepha never succeeded in competing with them for her mother's love. When she was in their company she always felt that she was playing the role of Cinderella. Her special bond with her father was her consolation for this. It was her father who took care of her from early childhood, fulfilling all her needs. The story which had been conveyed to Josepha was that it had been a big disappointment to her father that she was a girl; he wanted a son to bear his late father's name. During childhood and adolescence, Josepha and her father acted out the fantasy that she was her father's son; she even answered faithfully to the name Joseph, which was her grandfather's name.

At the age of six Josepha began accompanying her father to work on the farm. At first she was assigned easy tasks, which were soon replaced by time-consuming, burdensome ones. Josepha would get up before dawn to feed the chickens or do some other chores on the farm, while her sisters, who were 'mother's daughters', were considered the feminine type and thus spared hard labour. Josepha recalled her farm work with mixed feelings. At first she liked it – she could spend a lot of time with her father; she was also liked by the other labourers on the farm. Later, the long, tedious hours of physical labour together with her schoolwork placed great demands on her strength. She remembered her childhood as a story of exploitation, anger and bitterness. Josepha became angry with her father while doing her utmost to please him. Her father played both the maternal and paternal role. He sang lullabies to her, shortened her dresses, bought her intimate apparel, an so on. He also told her stories about a remote past in another country, and about his longing for his own father who had died shortly after he left home.

In her father's stories, her grandfather travelled frequently for business, while her father would wait for him to return. When Josepha grew up and went out with friends, she would return to find her father waiting for her at the intersection of the main road and the road to the farm. Josepha felt that her father was anxious to see her but, at the same time, expected to lose her, thus somehow repeating the experience with his own father.

During this period, Josepha was chronically late (fifteen–twenty minutes) to her sessions. By being late, she was acting out her omnipotent game with death (her disappearance) and revival (her reappearance). In this game, she fulfilled the double role of the father/child who disappears, and then miraculously comes back to life. By acting as the missing father, she tried to assign me the role of the helpless child who fearfully and angrily waits for his omnipotent parent to return. As my missing child, she attempted to make me feel the agony of a parent whose child has disappeared. Both father and child were miraculously brought back to life by her arrival for the session. In spite of her warm relationship with her father, Josepha nevertheless described her childhood as a game of hide-and-seek with death, connected to the father–child relationship. She illustrated this with morbid episodes in which fantasy and reality merged.

One of Josepha's favourite pastimes was to risk being shot at by a neighbour. This neighbour was irritated by the stray cats which inhabited his farm. When he heard their mewing, he would pick up his gun and shoot at them unhesitatingly. Josepha would sometimes hide behind bushes and 'meow' in order to provoke him. The man would come out of his house cursing the cat, and fire into the bushes, barely missing her.

This episode is an illustration of the theme of Josepha being killed by the loved–hated father which, later in analysis, we were able to understand as a reversal of her own death-wishes towards him.

In the transference, Josepha feared her destructive power and warned me against it. On the other hand, she projected upon me her own punitive super-ego, while fearing my retaliation. In the therapeutic relationship, she attacked me for being insensitive to her pain, distant, and 'too normal' to understand her. She would not let me speak, but would cut me off sharply, rejecting my inter-pretations as irrelevant. She was late with her payments, and attempted to pay her debts in small amounts over a long period of time. We both understood that the unconscious fantasy behind her wish to split the fee into insignificant fragments was to chop her analyst's value into worthless bits. She was thus attempting to relate to me in the same manner that she related to her own devalued self.

Analysing Josepha's murderous wishes towards me in the trans-ference led to the revelation that she had held the same wishes towards her paternal object. Josepha was finally able to share with me her deep conviction that her father's fatal heart condition had been caused by her hatred and destructiveness. She connected his first heart attack, which occurred while she was still in high school, to the fact that he couldn't stand the pace of her work. 'He cursed me and said I was bringing him death', Josepha said. 'He dug his own grave.' When her father had a second heart attack, Josepha's worst fantasies were actualised. She did not allow herself to feel guilty, but instead projected her own murderous wishes upon her father – 'He was always waiting for something terrible from me. Death was always there between us.'

The father's health deteriorated, and several years later, when he was close to death, he expressed the desire that Josepha, who was married by then, should have a child before he died. Josepha obeyed and became pregnant, her unconscious fantasy being that this would be her 'father's child'. Her father died during the pregnancy and Josepha never really mourned him. Like her own father, she gave the girl her father's name, thus actualising her omnipotent fantasy of bringing him back to life.

Enquiring about the tragic accident which occurred when her first daughter was four months old, I learned that it had happened several days before the first anniversary of her father's death. Thus, her father's death and the death of the child bearing his name became inseparably linked. In her unconscious fantasies, Josepha had 'killed' her father a second time. Josepha wished for her own death, but felt she was a prisoner of life, carrying the burden of a crime against both father and child. She shared with me a myriad of magical omnipotent ideas which connected the 'murder' of the father with that of the child. She believed that, by means of the accident, her father had taken revenge on her for her 'murderous' act against him; he was waiting for her with the angel of death behind him, attempting to strike her. Inadvertently, he struck her child and left her alive, thus handing her the ultimate punishment. It became clear to me that Josepha was using magical omnipotent ideas as a defence against the feelings of mourning and guilt which could have been overwhelming for her.

At this point in analysis I began to prepare Josepha for my forth-coming vacation. She reacted to our separation with a vivid memory from her childhood. When she was six years old, her mother left her for a period of six months to travel to the US in order to visit the sister whom she had never met. Josepha felt abandoned by her mother and neglected by her father, who was very busy with the farm at that time. She stopped eating and lost so much weight that her life was in peril. Only her mother's return helped her gradually to recover.

In the transference, we attempted to work through how vital analysis was for Josepha, and the life-threatening quality she attributed to our separation.

Phase IV – The revivification of feelings of pain and guilt

Josepha's aggressive, destructive reactions to my 'abandonment' appeared only after we resumed treatment, when she attempted to actualise in the transference the traumatic events which were reactivated by our separation.

First, Josepha launched a series of destructive attacks upon me as well as upon the therapeutic relationship. She made a sudden decision to interrupt analysis for the period of one month, claiming that she had to 'concentrate her efforts' on a final exami-nation. I tried in vain to relate her desire to leave analysis to her feelings of anger and retaliation against me, caused by our separation. She rejected my interpretation and 'disappeared', not turning up for the next session. She arrived two weeks later, only after I had 'searched' for her with several phone calls. Back in analysis, we discussed her claim that she 'had never left analysis'. In her mind, analysis had continued all along, and would have continued in that way had I not called and made her aware of the reality of what she had done. Actually, she came to inform me that now, due to financial difficulties, she could not continue analysis on a regular basis.

Instead of four times a week, she 'offered' to come to sessions twice a month. Josepha stressed her 'inability to kill relationships' as the main reason for her wish to retain a 'thread' of analysis. Listening to Josepha's proposal, I became aware of feelings of anger and frustration welling up inside me. I felt the deadly blow that Josepha was directing against me as well as against the therapeutic relationship. She wanted to turn me into a 'thread', weak and inefficient, and to make analysis a meaningless fragment of her life.

I refrained, however, from acting upon impulse and rejecting Josepha's 'offer'. Instead, I asked her to come for several sessions so that we could better understand the meaning of her request. During the ensuing sessions, I became aware of the importance of my 'staying alive' for her, which meant avoiding falling into her trap of retaliation by 'murdering' the therapeutic relationship. My refusal to see her on her terms would mean my disappearing from her life at the moment that she attempted to 'kill' me (her father), thus playing upon her omnipotent fantasy of being a murderess. A fragment from Josepha's words illustrates this: 'I've noticed this book you have on your shelf – *The Brothers Karamazov*, this is before *Crime and Punishment*. Somebody committed parricide, but this is true about all sons, isn't it? Who is the person who has never wanted to kill his father?' Only later in analysis were we able to connect her aggressive act against me to her abandonment by the other primary love object (her mother) in her childhood.

The inquiry into the unconscious wishes and fantasies behind Josepha's special request led to an understanding of its symbolic meaning. We connected the period of four months, during which she had requested to see me sporadically, to the age of her baby when she was killed in the car accident. We discovered that Josepha had intended to come back to analysis on the fatal week of the month in which she lost her father and her baby. I realised that Josepha, in the role of the child, had to come back to analysis and find that I was still there for her, alive and well, in spite of her efforts to destroy me.

I agreed, therefore, to see her sporadically over the next four months, after which we were to resume analysis on a regular basis. Josepha was flooded with relief. For the first time, she was able to express feelings of gratitude.

Josepha resumed regular analysis on the appointed date. There was a change in her attitude towards analysis as she accepted realistic boundaries of time and payments. Josepha expresses this in the following way: 'Today when I came to you I saw a funny advertisement on a billboard. Its title was "I got lost". It was about a limping puppy, whose owners took her to get x-rayed and then it got lost. A terrible story. Whoever finds a puppy with crooked legs, like mine, should help her to come back.' During the following year we attempted anew to work through her aggressive wishes towards her father in light of the transference relationship. Josepha began differentiating between the fantasy of her father punishing her by killing her child and the reality of the tragic accident. She no longer believed that the accident was caused by his retaliation for what she had done to him. 'That was only a fantasy', she explained to me.

Her crippling defences were giving way to feelings of mourning and guilt. For the first time, Josepha was able to cry. She mourned her lost baby, relating to it as a lost part of her own self. She referred to her love for her second daughter, attempting to differentiate between the live child and the departed one by saying, 'This is a new life, a new story.'

We attempted to understand the feelings of emptiness and psychic numbness which she had complained about at the start of analysis. She was now able to connect the feeling of being abandoned by me to her distressing memories of her mother. Thus, the mother's painful narrative of the Holocaust began to emerge.

Josepha had been conceived and born under unusual circumstances. When the Second World War ended, her mother heard rumours that her relatives (mother, brothers and their families) had perished in concentration camps. She became very depressed and reacted with body and soul. She developed terrible headaches as well as feelings of depersonalisation and derealisation. During that year, she became pregnant with Josepha and, in contrast to her past abortions, decided to bear this child.

Josepha was told that her mother's physical and mental state deteriorated markedly after her birth.

In analysis, Josepha described the 'big hole' she perceived in herself from an early age. She felt that the hole was caused by her mother's lack of interest in her survival. She had experienced herself as non-existent (a hole) for her mother, who was then very pre-occupied with the death of her relatives. Her mother felt especially guilty towards her own mother who, she thought, had been abandoned by all of her children to be murdered by the Nazis. When Josepha was six, her mother was visited by a woman from her home town who informed her of the fate of her relatives. She learned that her brothers and their families had indeed perished in concentration camps, but her mother had died peacefully of old age before the German invasion.

This information made Josepha's mother decide to leave her family for six months and travel to the US to meet her older sister, the only other surviving member of the family. Josepha remained at home with her father who was very busy with the farm. It was during this period that she stopped eating, sometimes slipping out of the house and hiding during mealtimes, but no one looked for her. We were now able to understand her 'hiding' from me when she 'disappeared' from analysis, and her manipulating me into searching for her. Josepha was able to realise that she linked food, survival and analysis into one vital knot.

Josepha attempted to work through her relationship with her internal maternal object. She described her mother's personality as fragmented, recounting three different images of her mother and giving each a different name. The first image was of a woman who catered to normality, for whom the outside world was very important. This mother was experienced by Josepha as coercive and false, pushing her towards 'being like the others'. This was the image Josepha had projected upon me in the transference at the beginning of therapy. The 'second' mother was the unpre-dictable, insane one who would not adhere to any rules. Josepha confessed that many times in the past she thought that, under my façade of normality, I was 'wild' and unruly.

Josepha's mother had never accepted the loss of her relatives and believed in their survival, a belief she tried to convey to her children. Similarly, Josepha perceived me as struggling to convince her that she was not dead, but was able to feel again.

The most painful relationship for Josepha was the one with the mother as a stranger (whom Josepha named 'she'), a wasteland devoid of feelings. Josepha described a woman she had recently seen stealing food from a restaurant. She was crazy, old, with a 'big hole on the side of her head'. 'This woman could have been my mother', she said. 'This woman is me.' This was the very 'hole' which she had introjected and which she had once believed could not be filled.

In the transference, Josepha became aware of her longing to fill the void in her heart with the warm feelings offered to her in analysis. We began to work through the guilt connected to her unconscious fantasy that she had destroyed her mother by being born. Josepha was grateful to me not only for surviving her aggression, but also for allowing her to be born emotionally in analysis, without feeling that she was injuring me in the process. During this period, the theme of being reborn recurred in her dreams. The following is a typical dream: Josepha was sliding down a hill towards a lake with blue water, while her mother remained seated behind her. Down in the lake she gave birth to a child; she then emerged from the water with the baby. We connected this dream to Josepha's desire to fill the 'hole' in herself by giving birth to the child aspect within herself in analysis. Josepha referred to her daughter as representing this newly-born aspect of herself. She described her as pretty and intelligent, with well-developed verbal skills. In the transference, I pointed out the change in her manner of communicating with me. We were both aware that Josepha had used the long journey in analysis to find and unlock the gate to her imprisoned feelings.

Discussion

I would now like to explore: (a) the phenomenon of psychic pain resulting from object-loss; (b) the inability of the sufferer to be in touch with her pain; and (c) the restoration of the capacity to feel pain and guilt as a result of the emotional experience in analysis.

(a) *Psychic pain resulting from object-loss.* Freud considered psychic pain to be a phenomenon parallel to physical pain. He outlined a theory of pain in the 'Project for a scientific psychology' (Freud, 1895) and in 'Inhibitions, symptoms and anxiety' (Freud, 1926, Addendum C). In the project, Freud defined pain as the consequence of a breach in the protective shield.

Freud also considered psychic pain to be a reaction to the loss of an object and connected it to anxiety. He believed that in psychic as well as in physical pain, the 'economic' conditions are the same: the libidinal energy (cathexis) invested in the longing which is concentrated upon the lost object and which causes anxiety is similar to the libidinal energy invested in the injured part of the body, which leads to pain. The prolonged nature of the above psychic process and the impossibility of halting it produce a state of mental helplessness which is similar to the helplessness induced by overwhelming pain. Thus, we can understand the painful character of object-loss (Freud, 1926, Addendum C).

Grinberg (1964) also referred to the connection between physical and psychic pain. He believed that if pain appears in any mourning situation as a result of object-loss, it is because object-loss is experienced by the unconscious fantasy as an attack upon the body-ego; this attack provokes physical pain, which in turn is experienced as psychic pain.

Joffe and Sandler (1965) pointed out an additional aspect of psychic pain connected to object-loss. They considered psychic pain to be the discrepancy between the actual state of the self and an ideal state of well-being. When a love object is lost, we not only lose the actual object, but also lose that aspect of our own self which is the complement in us of that object, as well as the well-being that is intimately bound up with it.

Pontalis (1981) also felt that psychic pain is connected to object-loss. Pain stems from the fact that the object is irrevocably lost but eternally retained: 'Where there is pain, it is the absent, lost object that is present; it is the actual, present object that is absent.'

(b) *The inability of the sufferer to be in touch with her pain.* In the case described here, the patient used psychic numbing as a defence against her unbearable feelings of pain and guilt. Such feelings stem from situations where actual traumas (the loss of the child) are associated with an underlying fantasy of hatred and destructiveness (towards the father). This impairs the work of mourning and leads to turning the aggression against the self.

Greenacre (1967) pointed out that, in situations where actual traumatic experiences are associated with an underlying fantasy stemming from difficult experiences, the impact of the actual trauma is more intense and the tendency to fixation is greater than in instances where life experiences were bland and incidental. That is why Josepha's father's illness and death, which were perceived by her as the actualisation of her omnipotent destructive fantasies, led to unbearable feelings of pain and guilt. Since she was not able to complete her mourning, Josepha not only attempted to bring her father back to life through her child, but she herself became the father (Freud, 1917). Her aggressive wish towards her father was subsequently deflected towards herself.

Josepha's aggressive feelings towards her mother were expressed in her fragmented self, her rejection of reality and her preoccupation with death. The 'hole' in her mother's psyche became her own. (This 'hole' was probably also the expression of Josepha's anaclitic depression caused by her mother's impaired holding ability during the first year of Josepha's life.) The aggression towards her mother was deflected towards herself and was expressed by the wish to starve herself to death during the mother's absence.

Another mechanism used by Josepha as a 'substitute for mourning' was the phenomenon of concretisation (Bergmann, 1982). Instead of being in touch with feelings of mourning and pain, she lived out her fantasies about her parents' past, and tried to recreate them in her own life. These fantasies contained unconsciously expressed themes of the original trauma: the act of bestowing her late father's name on her child symbolised bringing the father back to life, since, by being given the father's name, the child became the father (Gampel, 1986); the tragic accident symbolised the injuring of her father perpetuated upon her own body and that of her child. We can see Josepha's wish to die when her mother travelled abroad, as well as Josepha's accident as the actualisation of her parents' unconscious conflicts and fantasies connected to their own survival-guilt. The concretisation of her wishes pointed to a confusion between self and object, past and present, fantasy and reality.

(c) *The restoration of the capacity to feel pain and guilt.* The patient was unable to bear feelings of pain and guilt because they were associated with her feelings of hatred and her destructive wishes. She connected the loss of her baby to a series of events which appeared to her to be the actualisation of her aggressive wishes towards primary objects.

Freud (1920) referred to the polarity between love and hate with regard to a loved person, connecting it to 'the great opposition between the life and death instinct'. Riviere (1955) further developed this idea, adding that the loss and absence of loved objects can be equivalent in our unconscious to lack of love, hostility, hate, even malevolence, from them to us and in us to them. She expressed this in the following poetic way: 'Deep in the dynamic reservoir of instinctual forces, in the id, Eros, the life force and Thanatos, the death force are in never-ending strife, one always aiming at ascendancy over the other. Whether in absence, or in death, or in other situations of estrangement, the intolerable fear rises that it is our own deadly hate which brings about the loss; and the greater is the love, the more hate is feared' (Riviere, 1955, p. 364).

Thus, it was Josepha's love and need for her father that made her perceive herself as a murderess. This became traumatic when reality lent credence to those fantasies by means of the tragic accident in which her child was killed. Kris (1956) considered the distillation of the experiences over the course of one's life as the factor which determines which experience might gain significance as a traumatic one. The trauma made Josepha feel that the only punishment fit for her murderous deed was her own self-destruction.

Josepha felt guilty towards her mother for as long as she could remember. Her mere existence was reason for guilt, since her birth had caused the deterioration of her mother's fragile health. Her guilt feelings were reinforced at the age of six by her mother's long absence. Her unconscious aggressive wish towards her mother was fulfilled by her mother's disappearance, which was experienced by Josepha as death. Starving to death was the punishment that she inflicted upon herself.

Thus, both her father's illness and subsequent death and her mother's abandonment were perceived by Josepha as the actualisation of her aggressive wishes, reaffirming her belief in her destructiveness and her search for punishment.

During the course of analysis, unconscious feelings of pain and guilt were reactivated in the transference. Josepha's reaction was an aggressive attack on the therapeutic relationship, launched through an episode of acting out[6] (her wish to abandon therapy). By trying to destroy the therapeutic relationship, she attempted to 'murder' the father-analyst, and thus actualise her destructive fantasies during treatment. At the same time she tried to destroy the mother-analyst for abandoning her (feelings which were reactivated by our separation).

By surviving her fantasised destruction and not letting her ruin the therapeutic relationship, the analyst did not yield to Josepha's omnipotent fantasy of being a murderess. As a result of this experience, Josepha's feelings of omnipotence diminished and she perceived herself as less destructive; she began to differentiate between reality and her infantile aggressive wishes and fantasies (Kogan, 1989a).

Josepha's feelings of pain and guilt became bearable once they became dissociated from her hatred and her destructive wishes (Winnicott, 1964). She could therefore face depression without overwhelming feelings of anxiety and make some adaptations to reality (Balint, 1952).

V From Acting Out to Words and Meaning[7]

> *'Now I know what frightened him. I know that he felt guilty. And I also know that he was wrong. Who do I know this from? From myself, that's who. From myself, his son. For we resemble one another. I carry within me his past and his secret.'*
>
> E. Wiesel (1986)

I would like to explore and illustrate the behavioural phenomenon of concretisation (Bergmann, 1982) which was described in the introductory chapter to this book, and which, according to Bergmann, is characteristic of Holocaust survivors and their offspring. This phenomenon, which has repeatedly left an impression upon me in my own clinical work (Kogan, 1987, 1989a, 1989b, 1990, 1991, 1993) as well as in that of my colleagues, refers to fantasies which are lived out, grafted upon the environment and woven into current reality, rather than verbalised. It is particularly apparent in the early stages of analysis of patients whose parents underwent massive traumatisation and then denied their experiences. These children, in their endless efforts to understand and help their traumatised parents, try to experience what the parents went through by re-creating their parents' experiences and accompanying affects in their own life.

I would like to illustrate this phenomenon with material from the analysis of a young man suffering from psychotic episodes who shot and wounded his father during the latter's attempt to save him from suicide. Concretisation was a major element of this violent deed.

The working through of this episode was made possible by elaboration of the transference relationship, in which the patient repeated the destructive attack both against the analyst (by tem-

87

porarily breaking off the therapeutic relationship), as well as against his own self (in the form of psychosis). The analytic experience helped the patient realise the unconscious meaning of his actions and work through conscious and unconscious processes of identification, which led to the emergence of a separate sense of self.

Case Illustration

I became acquainted with Isaac, then aged twenty-two, in my role of clinical psychologist of the locked ward of a state mental hospital. The tragic incident which led to his hospitalisation was a suicide attempt during which he shot and wounded his father.

The background to this incident was as follows. Two years earlier, Isaac had suffered from psychotic depression, and he dropped out of college. His condition improved with psychiatric help, which consisted of a rehabilitation programme for young adults on an out-patient basis. After his recovery, he was drafted into the army, where he functioned reasonably well for the first two years. He then again became depressed and found it increasingly difficult to function within the army framework and to perform routine tasks. Recognising the symptoms of impending illness, he was torn between his desire to seek help and his self-destructive wishes which stemmed from his despair.

One night, in the midst of this conflict, alone in his army office, he telephoned his father on impulse, and told him that he was about to kill himself. His father begged him not to, and promised to come immediately. Isaac waited for him with a loaded gun in his hand. The father arrived to find a locked door. He pounded on the door and called out to his son, but there was no answer. In panic, he broke into the room together with a guard. In the ensuing noise and confusion, Isaac pulled the trigger. The father was shot and wounded in the arms and hands, and Isaac's thumb was injured by a bullet. The guard escaped injury.

As a result of this incident, Isaac was committed to a state mental hospital, and his father was taken to a general hospital for treatment of his wounds.

Phase I – The fragmented self behind the broken finger

At the beginning of his hospitalisation, Isaac was ruminative and negativistic. He felt that committing him to the hospital was a mistake, that the doctors did not understand his plight, that the patients around him were primitive and crazy.

It was decided that Isaac would not be treated with medication. Instead, he was referred to me for dynamic psychotherapy, which he willingly agreed to.

The content of our therapeutic sessions revolved around Isaac's feelings of disgust with his body. He felt that he had recently become fat, his muscles had become flabby, and his wounded thumb, despite several operations, was twisted. He felt that he could not continue living with such a finger. I was aware from all of this that Isaac was expressing psychotic anxiety.

In therapy, Isaac attempted to ignore my existence. He never addressed me, but rather sat sullenly, talking to himself. My repeated attempts at intervention fell on deaf ears. Session after session, while Isaac revelled in an orgy of self-hate, I felt that he was attempting to destroy any ray of hope I had for him. Realising that at this stage of therapy Isaac would not be able to tolerate any interpretations of his destructive wishes towards me and himself, I adopted a stance of neutral but empathic observer.

During this period, my countertransference reactions were the only possible foundation I had for working with him. On this basis, I formulated the following working hypotheses:

(a) Wounding and disabling his father as a result of his hatred and destructiveness had overwhelmed Isaac's ego and induced a state of psychic shock. In this state of mind he was completely incapable of being in touch with feelings of guilt and pain.

(b) Isaac was using massive projective identification to communicate to me, in a non-verbal manner, his feelings of loneliness and despair. I believed that this might have been a mode of communication familiar to him from his childhood.

(c) Isaac was suffering from anxiety which prevented him from developing an emotional attachment to me; his wounded finger possibly symbolised his impaired self, as well as his castrated masculinity. Perhaps he feared that by becoming close to me emotionally he would turn into a woman. This may also have been the reason that he couldn't tolerate interpretations, since he experienced them as penetrations, and he had a concrete fear of being penetrated and turned into a woman.

During this period, the only sign of Isaac's working alliance with me was the fact that he came willingly and punctually to his sessions. After several months of interminable ruminations, as my reservoir of hope was beginning to drain, Isaac reported a dream. In his dream, he left the session and saw that his finger was healing. In his associations regarding the dream, Isaac connected the healing of his finger to the therapeutic process. He expressed the hope that he, like his injured finger, would recover. He also told me that he had informed the staff on his ward that he appreciated me. I felt then that the long, arduous hours we had spent together had not been in vain. Here was the beginning of basic trust, upon which our future therapeutic alliance could be built.

During the latter part of Isaac's hospitalisation, several important events occurred. Isaac had never enquired about his father's fate. He was now told that his father had been wounded by him and was being treated in hospital. He was also informed that his father wanted to see him and he accepted this invitation without a display of emotion. However, I was later told by staff members who accompanied him on his visit to his father that a moving encounter had taken place between father and son. The father embraced his son with his wounded arms, expressing his forgiveness.

In therapy, Isaac rejected any attempt to uncover his feelings towards his father. This became possible only much later in analysis. Isaac was discharged from hospital with the recommendation that he receive further treatment in the army, and so was given the opportunity to complete his army service. Despite his enormous fears about his ability to be on his own and finish his service, Isaac accepted the challenge. Our imminent separation was met with denial of any feelings of anger or hurt.

Phase II – The lost self

It was due to the feelings of basic trust which we had established that Isaac came to me for analysis a year and a half later.

During the first interview, he expressed his urgent desire for treatment and described the events of the past year. He had completed his army service, which bolstered his self-esteem. He had a girlfriend, and the relationship was important to him. In spite of these achievements, he had a strong fear of losing control. He was afraid to live on his own, still living with his parents, upon whom he was dependent but did not get along with. After his release from the army he did not return to his studies and did not get a job.

In this interview I found that Isaac had changed for the better. He was more communicative and better able to express his feelings. He told me that our therapeutic relationship had been very meaningful to him; it had provided him with the strength and courage to go on living during a very difficult period of his life. I also learned that our separation had been interpreted by him as abandonment, and for some time he felt rejected and angry. He had not continued treatment in the army as recommended, but had found help and understanding in his relationship with his officers who were supportive.

I was impressed by Isaac's progress and his desire for further therapy. I stressed, however, that I would not accept him for analysis unless he found a job so that he could pay for treatment himself. Isaac felt this to be a major difficulty.

Shortly after this interview, Isaac called and announced that he had found a job in a local factory and was eager to commence treatment. He was intent on proving to both of us that he was highly motivated to do his share of the hard work ahead of us.

The beginning of analysis contrasted sharply with the somewhat optimistic picture of the initial interview. It revealed a glum image of Isaac, reminiscent of the person I had known at the hospital. Isaac was living in a barren, empty world where emotional response had been totally split-off. He completely avoided feelings of love, ambivalence and guilt. The sessions consisted of a tedious rundown of his daily routine, accompanied by a detailed description of his incomprehensible mood swings.

In the here-and-now of the analytic sessions I felt helpless and lost, drowning in a conglomeration of details which were the unconscious result of Isaac's aggression towards me. On the basis of our previous acquaintance, I knew that this was his way of conveying his feelings of despair and loss of self. As his condition had definitely improved since his release from hospital, I felt that he might now be able to tolerate an interpretative approach without too much anxiety or disintegration. I therefore pointed out to him what I believed was the unconscious wish behind his aggression. I suggested that by attempting to drown me in his sense of futility and lack of meaning he was testing my strength, his underlying wish being to lean upon me and thus ease the heavy burden of grief and guilt bearing down upon him.

Isaac listened to me quietly; he seemed to be looking inwards, searching into himself. He then reacted to my interpretation with an outburst of emotion; for the first time allowing himself to cry. At long last, his obsessive, meaningless ruminations gave way to the expression of wishes and fantasies. These consisted of infantile longings to be cared for (such as being fed and protected by me), mixed with powerful oedipal desires. In his fantasies, Isaac was my child and my lover, feeling guilt, shame and anger regarding his incestuous longings. The attempt to work through Isaac's libidinal and aggressive wishes towards me in the transference led to the discovery of his complex, painful relationship with representations of primary objects.

Isaac was the only son of a family with a low socio-economic background. His mother had married very young, after running away from home because her parents would not consent to her marriage. She was poorly educated and worked hard as a seamstress to help support the family. The father was a Holocaust survivor who came to Israel in his late teens, together with his mother. The father's father, after whom Isaac was named, perished in the Holocaust, at the beginning of the war. In Israel, the father first worked as a manual labourer in a factory, but over the years learned carpentry and now owned his own shop.

Isaac described his complex relationship with a combined mother figure – which included his mother, his paternal grandmother and his aunt (his mother's sister), all of whom had had a great impact on the formation of his personality. He referred to his mother, to whom he was very attached, as a lonely, unhappy woman. The mother did not regard her husband as a partner with whom to share her life, but instead turned to her only son for love and satisfaction.

On the one hand, Isaac claimed that he had done everything he could to make his mother happy: he strove to obtain good grades in school, sang in the school choir and danced in a youth group; he tried to be successful for her. In the transference, Isaac talked about his efforts to find work in order to satisfy me. On the other hand, Isaac resented being his mother's partner and feeling responsible for her well-being. In analysis, Isaac complained, 'I'm doing so much for you; I'm working my ass off in order to pay for these sessions. I know I have to pay, but it all seems unfair to me.'

From the age of three months, Isaac was cared for by his paternal grandmother, who lived in his parents' house until his adolescence. Isaac's mother returned home from work only in the evening, so, essentially, the grandmother fulfilled the role of mother; she fed and protected him and he was very attached to her. He often felt torn and guilty because of the quarrels between her and his mother.

Isaac remembered that at mealtimes his grandmother would often tell him stories about a remote past and about the wonderful grandfather whose name he bore. The grandmother was in poor health and sometimes lay in bed for days, complaining about her pains and crying. At those times, Isaac feared she might die and leave him. He often felt guilty, thinking that his disobedience was the reason for her suffering.

In analysis, Isaac related a story that he had read about a child who was brutally murdered. The murderer tore open the child's stomach, took out his guts and fed them to him. I was aware from this story that Isaac expected and feared my sadistic retaliation for his destructive wishes towards me. He was afraid that I would wring out the inner meaning of his deeds and feed him those thoughts and ideas which he had chosen not to know, thus bringing about his destruction.

During this period, Isaac expressed longings for the boundless, unconditional love he had experienced as a child. He resented the realistic boundaries of analytic therapy. 'I don't understand why I have to stick to these damned four hours a week: sometimes I feel the need to return to you five minutes after I've left; other times I just hate the idea of coming here at all. Why can't I be with you for as long as I want, whenever I feel like it?'

In the transference, I felt that Isaac was behaving like a ravenous, aggressive baby. He was not only clinging and demanding, but actually tried to threaten me by being so emotionally needy. A violent incident heightened my awareness of the concrete nature of his fantasies and his shaky hold on reality. At the end of one session, Isaac simply refused to leave. 'What will you do if I don't go away in spite of everything you say?', he asked provocatively. 'I don't give a shit about your next patient.' For several moments we were silent, and I felt fear creeping over me. 'Listening' to my fear, I said quietly, 'I will be here for you next session. Don't be so afraid.' Isaac got up and smiled. 'OK, I'm going then', he said.

This incident made me aware of my fear of Isaac, of the violent nature of his acting out. But I also realised that the source of my fear must have been his terror of developing an emotional attachment to me. He had projected this fear onto me and I identified with it. This realisation was reinforced by a dream he reported during the next session. In his dream, Isaac saw a naked woman dancing in front of a child. She was an older woman, and her body was far from perfect. When the child approached her, a tremendous vagina opened up in front of him, and the child was almost swallowed into her. In his associations regarding the dream, Isaac talked about the way he had experienced his mother during his childhood. His mother would roam around the house in her underwear, and he found her physical closeness loathsome. Later, as an adolescent, he used to masturbate in her bed.

The tremendous vagina in the dream reminded him of his timidity and his shrinking away from women until his present girlfriend. For a long time he had believed that he would never be able to perform the sexual act. He was always astonished when women praised his good looks. It seemed to him that they were talking about a stranger; he felt ugly and incompetent in the role of a man. At the next session, Isaac broke off in the middle of a sentence, saying he was too ashamed to describe what he was feeling. Only after I encouraged him to continue was he able to shamefacedly describe having an erection during the session. 'This is impossible, to have such feelings towards you', Isaac said. 'Sometimes I think that therapy will make me sick again, and then I'll be powerless, like in the past.' By working through his fear that I might break down his defences and make him insane, I realised that Isaac was using his oedipal feelings towards me as a defence against much deeper fears evoked by his emotional attachment to me, which he believed could lead to his loss of control and destruction. In his unconscious fantasies either he would hurt and damage me, or he would be devoured, incorporated and destroyed by me. This could be seen from his recollection of his crazy aunt, his mother's sister. Isaac knew that she suffered from a manic-depressive illness and that she had been hospitalised on and off. His mother kept him safely away from this aunt so that he wouldn't 'catch her illness'. In the transference, he assigned me the role of the dangerous, persecutory aunt, who might seduce him and then swallow him into her madness. The following story, which he told with a mixture of horror and gusto, illustrated this theme.

In a movie dealing with a wife's revenge on her husband for killing her lover, the woman prepared a ghastly feast. She cooked her dead lover in the oven, then served the full-size corpse to her husband, sticking a knife and fork into it. In the end, the woman ate her lover, so as to be united with him. In the transference,

Isaac expressed his fear of being devoured by me. He was my lover who could be punished in this dreadful manner for his incestuous wishes. Simultaneously, he was also the killer who wanted to destroy and swallow me. Working through the transference relationship, we were able to connect Isaac's fear of being devoured by me to his fantasy of being swallowed by his insane aunt. Only later in analysis were we able to relate his attempt to kill and incorporate his aunt to the dead bodies which he was 'fed' through his grandmother's stories and which, unconsciously, had become part of him.

At this point, Isaac tried to avoid developing becoming emotionally close to me through an episode of acting out. He was unfaithful to his regular girlfriend, sleeping with a younger girl from his factory, hinting that he wanted to take 'revenge' on me by showing that he could easily replace me with someone who could fulfil his sexual desires. But the enquiry into the unconscious fantasies and wishes underlying this manifest message led us again to the conclusion that his running away from me stemmed from his fear of losing his self in the relationship. Further proof of this fear came from his painful, complex relationship with his father. He expressed this fear in a dream which he reported with tremendous anxiety. In his dream, Isaac had undergone a metamorphosis and had become identical to his father – old, fat, unkempt and helpless. In the transference, Isaac felt that he was becoming identical to me. Isaac perceived me as weak and impotent because of my being a woman, which led to complaints about his own weakness and impotence. He expressed longings for a powerful male figure with whom he might identify, and who would bestow upon him the admired masculine attributes he felt he lacked.

The tragic reality at home reinforced Isaac's fear of seeing his own reflection in the image of his father. Life with his family had become unbearable due to the father's unsuccessful rehabilitation. The father had been unable to return to work because of his damaged hands and arms. Considered totally disabled, he became very depressed and would lie in bed for days, refusing to get up, dress and eat. Because of his deteriorating emotional condition, he was eventually hospitalised at the same mental hospital where Isaac had been committed. In the transference, I became aware that I was assigned the role of the weak, impotent father-analyst, and that Isaac's fear of becoming identical to me was increasing. These feelings provoked so much anxiety in him that he attempted

to destroy me (his image) by breaking the therapeutic relationship. He joined a bizarre religious sect based on Eastern
philosophies. There he became the subject of an almighty leader
who conducted painful, humiliating ceremonies and whose power
Isaac hoped to acquire through a spiritual union. Becoming
greatly obsessed with these religious ceremonies, he quit his job
and finally decided to leave analysis.

As a result of the deadly blow which Isaac was trying to direct
against our therapeutic alliance, I became aware of my feelings
of frustration and anger. In this situation, I felt powerless to
prevent him from destroying the relationship. I began to have
doubts about my role of analyst in this case and about the feasi-
bility of using analysis for a psychotic individual who was trying
to escape from the relationship with me by defensively destroying
it. It gradually dawned upon me that my feelings reflected Isaac's
attempts to 'wound my therapeutic arms', in the same way that
he had injured his father as he tried to save him from his self-
destructive attack. This led me to the further hypothesis that
Isaac was unconsciously attacking our therapeutic alliance in
order to test my ability to resist his aggression without being
destroyed myself. This hypothesis gave me the strength to resume
my therapeutic role. Thus, I suggested to Isaac that he come for
several sessions so that together we could examine his decision.
During these sessions it became clear that Isaac was adamant in
his desire to run away from me, since I had become the
embodiment of his own impaired self. I pointed out to him that,
in spite of his rejection, I would remain available to help him,
and that I expected him to come back to analysis in order to
continue the search for his own self. Isaac seemed greatly relieved;
he stood by his decision to leave analysis, but was also able to
express how much he loved me all along.

A couple of months later, Isaac suddenly burst unannounced
into my office, demanding to be seen immediately on an
emergency basis. He was very troubled and agitated, and only when
I agreed to see him shortly did he quiet down somewhat.

Isaac's appearance had changed greatly – he had grown a beard
and put on weight, which made him appear much older. I had a
fleeting thought that outwardly he had become identical to his
father, fulfilling the frightening wish expressed in his previous
dreams.

Once in my office, Isaac spoke incoherently about holy scriptures,
holy men, his fight with the devil. His speech was accompanied

by agitated movements. He tossed his head backwards and closed his eyes as if in a trance. In spite of his floridly psychotic condition, I gathered from Isaac that he had come for help.

I telephoned the hospital and arranged for Isaac's immediate hospitalisation. In contrast to his initially aggressive behaviour, he obediently accepted my decision. Isaac left, giving me his blessing. Only after he left did I realise that my knees were shaking and that I had been exposed to a possible attack. This was confirmed when I learned from the hospital that Isaac, upon arrival, had violently attacked the doctor on call. Later, I noticed that Isaac had left his identity card behind in my office and also a small notebook in which he had written a day-to-day description of his struggle with his oral and libidinal wishes during the time he had spent in the commune.

I realised that, through these two mementoes, Isaac had unconsciously left me a message that he would return to analysis to search for his lost identity.

Phase III – The search for the self

After a period of several months, Isaac phoned me and asked to come back to analysis. He told me he had been through a difficult time but felt much better now. His voice was calm and sober.

During the first session, Isaac mentioned that he had lost his identity card. During his stay in hospital he thought that he could use his father's card and nobody would notice. Seeing his father in the hospital was very confusing for him since he did not always know who was who. During this period in hospital, he had dreams in which he tried to run away from his sick, impaired father. In these recurring dreams, he was running through the forest trying to save himself from the Nazis, leaving a wounded father behind. On other occasions, he was the wounded father whose son was fleeing to save his life.

We attempted to understand Isaac's confusing himself with his father in light of the transference relationship. I suggested to Isaac that he must have felt confused about us too, since he had attempted to run away from me in analysis. For the first time, he tried to work through the fears he had had during the different phases of analysis of forming an attachment to me. At the start, Isaac said that he had felt very threatened by me since he felt totally empty, had no wishes, no initiative and felt the danger of becoming permeated with my ideas and values. The defence he erected against this was to try to ignore my existence. As the relationship

slowly evolved and I began to exist for him, it evoked the frightening feeling in him that we were identical. He felt that I was lost,
incapable of struggling with his plight, exactly like him. He
therefore abandoned me, thinking that only a powerful leader could
give him the strength he required.

It was very important for Isaac to recall all that had passed
between us. Isaac stressed that my reaction to his abandonment
had convinced him that I was different from him. He experienced
me as being stronger than he had thought, since I had given him
the opportunity to come back to treatment. I realised that this
dissipated his fear that he had damaged the relationship and
made him feel less guilty about his destructiveness.

In light of our therapeutic relationship, Isaac felt safe enough
to begin exploring the differences which existed between him and
his internal paternal object.

Isaac perceived his father as a primitive, uneducated and brutal
man; he had never gone to highschool and was obsessed with food
and money. At home he was always sullen and irritable. Isaac had
no memories of being emotionally close to him. As a child, he
had hated his father's moodiness and bouts of depression. He had
hated his parents' terrible quarrels even more. He always felt that
he had to protect his mother from his father's wrath and brutality.
He remembered the house of his childhood as old and decrepit,
literally falling apart.

Despite his education, youth and good looks, Isaac perceived
himself as similar to his father. He considered himself stupid and
ignorant. He despised his own greediness, stinginess and depressive
tendencies – his father's characteristics which were embedded in
himself.

For the first time, Isaac was ready to explore the terrible incident
in which he had wounded his father as well as himself. I suggested
to him the possibility that his attack upon his father, like his attack
upon me in analysis through his abandonment, was intended to
kill the father inside himself, from whom he had never really
separated. Isaac reacted to my interpretation by expressing his desire
to become better acquainted with his father. In contrast to the
past, he now felt that he would like to learn the concrete details
of his father's past, which were somehow connected to his grandmother's stories. My supportive attitude gave him the courage and
strength to do so.

To Isaac's great surprise, his father answered his questions
readily, as if he had been waiting a long time for this moment.

A story of grief and terror was unfolded before Isaac. Listening to it, he had the feeling that he had always known the story.

Isaac's father was an adolescent (an only child) when the Nazis occupied Poland. There ensued a period of terror, during which he and his parents hid in the house of gentile friends. One night, the Germans entered the house and caught the father while he and his mother hid in a closet in a nearby room. They interrogated the father about the other members of his family, then shot him. He and his mother heard everything from their hiding place – the brutal questioning, the choking panic and the painful death groan. After what seemed an eternity, they emerged from the closet and discovered the father's dead body lying in a pool of blood. They fled to the forest where they lived as fugitives for several years. This was why Isaac's father had never received any education. Isaac's father added that he was glad he had succeeded in saving Isaac from self-destruction in spite of his injury.

Isaac was dumbfounded by his father's story and especially by his last remark. In analysis, he tried to master the overwhelming feelings it had evoked in him.

It now occurred to Isaac that he had been avoiding his feelings towards his father for a long time. Disturbing, frightening questions came to his mind, such as: Why did he phone his father the night that he contemplated suicide? How was it possible that the bullets which were intended for himself were shot towards his father's arms and hands? Why did he feel that his father's story was something he had lived through himself?

We attempted to understand Isaac's questions in light of the transference relationship. We first examined the non-verbal way in which Isaac had communicated his feelings of guilt and depression to me. We realised that this kind of communication was familiar to him from childhood. 'I didn't have to look at him', said Isaac. 'I knew how he felt since I felt the same way.' I pointed out to Isaac that, on a certain level, his feelings of despair and helplessness, which had brought him close to suicide, might have belonged to his grandmother's and father's life; they might have been transmitted over the years through his grandmother's stories, as well as in non-verbal ways.

We further explored the possibility that, by attempting to kill his father as well as himself, Isaac might have been acting out different roles in the drama of his father's past. It is possible, said Isaac, that by calling him the night that he wanted to commit suicide, he was attempting to give his father the opportunity of becoming a saviour and thus expiate his lifelong guilt. I pointed out to Isaac the other possibility, that by wounding his father he was identifying with the Nazi aggressor who had killed the father's father and left the child to his own life of misery and guilt.

Thus we both understood that Isaac wanted to heal as well as to kill his internal paternal object. Through his destructive attack he had simultaneously fulfilled the roles of 'murderer' (by attempting to get rid of his father) and 'saviour' (by trying to alleviate his father's guilt feelings). The 'saviour' aspect of the father now became evident through an incident which caused Isaac much emotional turmoil. The father, whose condition had improved, returned home from hospital. He found a little dog which had been run over by a car and was badly injured, gave it shelter and food and saved its life. In the transference, Isaac felt that I had done the same thing for him. The discovery of his father's traumatic history and the working-through of its impact on his life were accompanied by an upsurge of feelings of guilt as well as love towards the father. On the way towards the consolidation of his newly-born sense of self, we embarked on the long journey of working through Isaac's feelings of guilt without the threat that he would be destroyed. Isaac also returned to an earlier theme of his emotional involvement with me as a maternal object. He was now able to work this through with less fear of his being swallowed and lost in the relationship. It was as if a psychic boundary had been established between us, enabling Isaac to continue analysis with a more secure sense of self.

Discussion

I would like to focus on one aspect of Isaac's destructive attack against his father – the phenomenon of concretisation. I would also like to explore the process leading to the stabilisation of Isaac's ego boundaries as a result of the analytic experience.

Concretisation

Isaac grew up in a home where the paternal grandmother had served as a substitute mother during his childhood. This woman, who was sickly and suffered from bouts of depression, had probably transmitted her story to Isaac both narratively and mimetically, through her behaviour. The perception of her traumatic experiences must have occurred in the early stages of Isaac's development.

This is perhaps what had led Isaac to feel that he shared his father's secret without having really known it, as if he had always been with his father, even before his own birth (Klein, 1973a).

The special bond between Isaac and his grandmother enhanced the permeability of his ego boundaries in those areas related to the trauma. Isaac became the outlet for his grandmother's immense, inextinguishable feelings of anxiety which she probably could not cope with and which she tried to deny. From a very young age, Isaac thrived on her stories which conveyed to him the message of living without ever forgetting the dead.

Introjecting this message, he was destined to become those who had perished (by being given his grandfather's name, he was to become his grandfather [Gampel, 1986a; Gampel, 1986b; Kogan, 1990]). The knowledge of traumatic experiences, which Isaac had introjected and repressed throughout the years, created in him the need to externalise the past and express psychic conflicts and fantasies in a concrete way.

However, it is my belief that concretisation through such a violent acting-out would not have occurred had Isaac not been suffering from a psychotic disturbance. Because he was psychotic, the means at the disposal of his ego to differentiate between self and object, inner and outer reality, as well as to tame and regulate his aggression, were poor. His capacity for fantasy was impaired by growing up with traumatised parental figures who denied their traumatic experiences (Grubrich-Simitis, 1984).

That is why Isaac could not deal with his grandmother's and father's experiences on a fantasy level alone. He was unable to control his sadistic wishes through the use of his imagination rather than through acting them out. He used concretisation in order to suppress his rage and anxiety and to achieve greater control over his father's and grandmother's traumatic experiences which he lived out as if they were his own story. The aspect of the concretised fantasy which we have elaborated upon during this stage of analysis contained unconsciously expressed themes of the original trauma; it symbolised the reanimation of the grandfather whose name Isaac bore (by Isaac becoming the grandfather) and his deanimation (killing him) at the same time. We were thus able to work through the splitting of his father's image into the 'saviour' and the 'murderer' and his identification with both roles through his acting out.

Concretisation serves as a mechanism for avoiding psychic pain, and it is similar to the type of phenomenon which the French school calls *pensée operatoire* (Marty and de M'Uzan, 1983). This phenomenon refers to a pragmatic way of thinking about people and events and a lack of emotional response to crucial moments or traumatic losses in the lives of the people concerned. Isaac's condition, when he was in an affectless state resembled the phenomenon of *pensée operatoire*.

Stabilisation of ego boundaries

The stabilisation of Isaac's ego boundaries was an outcome of the emotional experience in this later stage of analysis. Throughout this stage, Isaac tested my strength again and again. He had to feel that 'my analyst cannot be permeated by my hatred and aggression; she does not reject me, therefore we are different from each other'. In other words, Isaac had to perceive me as a separate person who could not be incorporated into himself. This diminished his fear of being swallowed by me in the relationship, and strengthened his sense of self. To quote Winnicott (1971) on this matter: 'In psychoanalytic practice, the positive changes that come about in this area can be profound. They do not depend on interpretative work. They depend on the analyst's survival of the attack, which involves and includes the idea of the absence of a quality of change to retaliation.' I believe that in this case it was my survival, together with the analytic understanding, that helped the patient.

In order to clarify the inner meanings hidden in his terrifying acting-out, Isaac took me on as a partner in his search for the concrete details of his father's past. By working through his attempt to break the therapeutic relationship, Isaac became aware of the unconscious meanings expressed in his suicide attempt – giving his father the opportunity to save him and getting rid of his father. This process enabled us to continue our analytic work and begin the working-through of Isaac's relationship with the maternal object with less fear of his getting lost in it.

The blurring of the boundaries between self and object representations threatens the self with annihilation (Jacobson, 1964; Kernberg, 1986). The purpose of this part of analysis was to annul this threat by enabling differentiation and restoring Isaac's capacity to feel guilt, love and ambivalence.

VI Love and the Heritage of the Past[8]

'The affirmation of one's own life, happiness, growth, freedom, is rooted in one's capacity to love.'

E. Fromm (1962)

Introduction

The capacity to fall and remain in love has been amply explored in psychoanalytic literature (Freud, 1912; Balint, 1948; May, 1969; Wisdom, 1970; Josselyn, 1971; Kernberg, 1976). In this chapter, I would like to examine this subject from a very specific angle – the impact of the traumatic past of Holocaust survivors on the love-life of their offspring.

If one had to choose a single aspect which characterises the difference between the analysis of Holocaust survivors' offspring and the analysis of others, it would be the problem of mourning. This chapter explores the relationship between the mourning process and the capacity to fall in love as it is revealed in a case study of a Holocaust survivor's daughter, whose mother lived through the Holocaust as a child.

I intend here to explore the relation between mourning processes and the capacity to fall and remain in love from two angles: (1) the relation between 'normal' mourning which is incurred in the process of growth and separation and the creation of love relationships; and (2) the relation between the denied mourning of survivor parents and the atrophy of the child's ability to love.

1.   Bergmann (1971) said that the capacity to love presupposes a normally developing symbiotic experience and an individuation-separation phase. Bak (1973) stressed the relation

between being in love and mourning, stating that being in love is an emotional state based on the separation of mother and child, and directed toward overcoming this as well as later separations and losses of important objects.

In cases of Holocaust survivors' offspring, these processes are often disturbed. In her exploration of the relationship between children of Holocaust survivors and their bereaved parents, Freyberg (1980) showed that Holocaust survivors' offspring tend to experience their bereaved parents as emotionally detached and tend to cling dependently to them, feeling incapable of going through the process of separating from them. In these cases, the child may often experience individuation as destructive towards his vulnerable parents, who cannot sustain any more 'losses' in their lives. The child tends to remain attached to the parents in a manner which does not allow him to leave them behind and work through the 'normal' mourning of separation when this is required to form a love relationship (Kernberg, 1974).

2.   Another element which contributes to the impairment in the capacity to fall and remain in love is the deprivation of the opportunity to mourn. Josselyn (1971) has suggested that parents who deprive the child of opportunities to mourn over the loss of loved objects contribute to the atrophy of the capacity to love. The reason for this is that a prerequisite for the capacity to love is the achievement of a stage of development where there is a capacity for mourning, guilt and concern, resulting in a deepening awareness of the self and of others, the beginning of the capacity for empathy and for higher level identifications. This links the development of the capacity to love with the capacity for and proneness to depression.

In cases of Holocaust survivors' offspring, parents often deny their own mourning for their dear lost ones, and deprive their children of the opportunity to mourn, thus bringing to an impairment in their capacity for empathy and ability to love.

In the light of the theoretical premises mentioned above, as well as in regard to the relationship with the traumatised mother which I will presently examine, I want to report a case study in which I will show that the patient's inability to love was a result of her inability to go through the necessary mourning processes connected to the separation from her bereaved mother, as well as of her fixation to the mother's interminable, denied mourning. In her paper, 'The impact of the Holocaust on the second generation', Pines (1993) expressed the opinion that the development of second-generation children is more affected if it is the mother, the first caretaker, who has sustained the losses, thus becoming incapable of providing a secure foundation for her baby.

In this case study, the patient's relationship with the damaged mother was often characterised by an intense, unconscious rage directed at her, which she protected herself against by losing her autonomous self through a process of 'primitive identification' (Freyberg, 1980; Grubrich-Simitis, 1984; Kogan, 1990, 1991). By identifying with the bereaved mother, a recathexis of traces of the trauma which have been transmitted to the daughter occurred, thereby intensifying the transmitted trauma and thus strengthening the neurotic pattern.

As a result of this recathexis, there was a need for 'concretisation' (Bergmann, 1982; Kogan, 1987, 1990, 1991, 1993), an attempt of the daughter to experience what she imagined her mother has been through in the Holocaust by re-creating her mother's experiences and the accompanying affects in her own life.

The recathexis of the transmitted trauma through the process of primitive identification and the need to concretise had an impact on the daughter's subsequent love relationships. She gave the love objects libidinal meaning by disconnecting them from the present and transforming them into actors in the drama which she imagined her mother went through in the past, a drama which the daughter found to be replete with libidinal meaning. This drama, which involved themes of rescue and death, was usually coloured with manic sadism because it was impossible for the daughter to direct her aggression at what she perceived as her vulnerable mother. The daughter who was fixated on her mother's traumatic past distorted the relationships with the objects and unconsciously exploited them to fulfil her need to act out her fantasies about her mother's traumatic past in her own life.

I will illustrate the distortion of object-relations and the daughter's need to play out the role of victim/persecutor in relation to her mother's imagined past, which impaired her capacity to fall and remain in love, with excerpts from analysis.

Case Illustration

Sara, an educational psychologist, sought help because of her unhappy love-life. Still single at thirty-eight, she had had a long list of partners. Her relationships did not last long. Men either left her because they lost interest in her, or were abandoned by her because of what she called her 'marriage anxiety'. Her emotional life in a mess, she felt she was different from other people and feared a lonely, childless future.

Sara had been in therapy for a period of one year with two different male therapists. She left therapy with an empty-handed feeling, which is how she always felt at the end of all of her previous relationships.

Sara filled my room with her stunning appearance. She was tall, slim, with a dark-complexioned, exotic, oriental beauty. She was elegantly dressed and appeared younger than her age. Sara seemed to me intelligent and eager for treatment. I suggested analysis (four times a week) as the treatment of choice, she accepted my suggestion with feelings of great expectation mixed with anxiety.

I do not intend to describe in detail all of the factors which influenced Sara's love-life, such as her inner representation of her father, the way she perceived the relationship between her parents, and so on – suffice to say that Sara perceived her father as a childish, castrated man, needing love and admiration from everybody, and dependent both physically and emotionally upon her mother. The fact that her father had been very successful in his profession and a good provider was belittled by Sara, who considered him weak and living in the shadow of her strong, dominant, talented mother. Sara perceived her mother as constantly criticising him and complaining about him, as if he were incapable of meeting her expectations.

I will illustrate the relationship between the mourning process and the capacity for falling and remaining in love by focusing on Sara's relationship with her mother.

During the first analytic sessions, I was able to form a hypothesis about the special nature of Sara's object-relations from the transferential picture she had created of me before coming for treatment. One of Sara's friends had recently attended a series of introductory lectures on psychoanalysis, which I gave at the psychology department of one of the universities. The department chairman was present and participated in the discussion. Sara claimed that her friend had portrayed me as an attractive woman who made fun of the department chairman with her sharp irony and sarcasm. Sara was intrigued by this description, and it led her to seek an appointment with me.

I was taken aback by what Sara wanted to find in me – a phallic, sadistic woman who squelches her male partner. Was this the way she expected me to treat her? Or was this Sara's own projection of herself on the mirror I provided for her in analysis? If so, was I already doomed to become the ineffectual, worthless analyst, like the therapists who preceded me?

At the beginning of analysis, Sara's anxiety mounted until it reached a climax. Sara perceived analysis, like marriage, as a 'limitless black hole' into which she could be swallowed and lost. Her central fantasy in this regard was her longing for, as well as her fear of, becoming a passive victim of torture and rape. 'Lying down for me is giving myself completely. Like – take this body and do something with it!' And later: 'You are putting your hand into the barrel and taking out things I didn't even feel I had.' Sara's aggressive wishes of incorporating me became twisted in the transference, turning her into my victim; she expected me to force her to swallow things she didn't want to swallow, because her need of me was so great. We can see this from her first dream, in which she was climbing a mountain in order to come to the session. At the top of the mountain there was a woman who offered her a glass of milk which tasted like ashes. Sara was thirsty and gulped it all down. In her associations regarding the dream, Sara said:

> I remember that as a child I could not eat, I was chewing the food on one side of my mouth and then moving it to the other side, never swallowing it. Mother was afraid I'd be so thin that I wouldn't grow up. When I did grow up I became too fat, and I had to diet to make Mother happy. I was always such a good girl, I can puke. Mother always wanted me to do things I did not want to do. She wanted me to have a different profession and a high position in the world. I had to get a 'perfect' husband of high status. I was never able to fulfil her expectations.

In the transference, I became this overpowering mother who pushed down her throat food she didn't want: 'You are so stubborn, in the end you'll lead me by the nose to some place I didn't want to be at all, maybe I'll do things in life I do not intend to do because of you.' On the other hand, Sara was afraid that by rejecting the spoiled food she expected from me she might lose my love: 'People are often disappointed in me', she said. 'I create expectations which I cannot fulfil. I'm afraid I'll let you down.'

Next session, Sara described a dream dealing with the rejection of food: 'There was a party with many people around, my little brother was there vomiting, and I told him: "Do vomit, get it all out of yourself!" And I felt sick too and I wanted to vomit. But I could not, all the vomit got stuck in my throat.' Sara's associations in regard to this dream were: 'Mother swallowed tons of shit. First they took away her father, then her mother. I cannot be angry with mother, I love her a lot.'

Working through these dreams, I helped Sara realise that the young brother in her dream symbolised her younger aspect who rejected the 'shit' she felt she had swallowed through her life. Her older self, in spite of his wishes, seemed incapable of doing this. I suggested to Sara that I felt she was not only afraid she would have to 'swallow' my needs and wishes and act upon them, but she expected me to also force her to 'vomit', to take out the angry feelings she harboured towards her beloved mother. In this way, I was expected to become the persecutor who brings about her separation from her mother.

After listening to Sara's dreams, my thoughts reverted to Sara's complex relationship with her mother: What was it, I wondered, that Sara was unable to swallow or vomit? Was it only her anger towards her beloved mother that was so difficult for her to bear? Or was it the unknown part in her mother's past, the part which was tainted with death, that made 'her mother's milk taste like ashes' and stick in her throat in a way that she could neither 'swallow' it (that is, integrate it into her unconscious self) nor reject it as belonging to her mother's life and not to her own?

Only later in analysis were we able to link Sara's dreams to her mother's story of her battered childhood, which had been introjected by Sara and played out in her life as if it were her own story. I will now present a brief description of the mother's traumatic history, which I believe had a tremendous impact on Sara's love-life.

Sara's mother lived through the Holocaust between the ages of nine and thirteen. Her father had been drafted into the army two years before the war and later disappeared in a concentration camp. Sara's mother hid for some time with her own mother (Sara's grandmother) and twin sister (Sara's aunt) until they were discovered and transported to a concentration camp. Shortly thereafter, two nuns arrived at the concentration camp with a local Bishop's permit to take away some of the children in order to save them. The mother encouraged her twin daughters to go with them. The mother herself stayed behind and perished in Auschwitz.

The twins were first taken to a convent located near the Gestapo headquarters, where they lived in terror of a possible raid. They were soon smuggled into another country, where they were separated and placed in different homes. Sara's mother did not get on with the people with whom she was staying. They mistreated and beat her. The story of her mother's journey was the source of many of Sara's persecutory fantasies. Sara vividly described the hungry children suffering from cold and terrified of being hung, like the people whose corpses her mother had seen dangling from the trees. Eventually, Sara's mother and her twin sister, who had a damaged leg, were taken by ship to Israel where they were raised in an orphanage for children who had survived the Holocaust.

Years later, the mother's sister developed a growth on her spine and had to undergo an operation which left her permanently crippled. The doctors, who had expected her to recover, raised the possibility that her illness might have been connected to the trauma she had suffered when escaping through the woods and injuring her leg.

In the first year of analysis, Sara's unconscious fantasy of being her mother's twin sister was revealed through a story about a cousin who gave birth to twins, one of whom died because the other 'sucked his blood'. The surviving twin became very sick. Through this story, I realised that Sara, in the role of Mother's twin partner, felt that her existence was lethal to her mother.

Sara's fear of the need to kill her mother (her twin) so that she herself would survive was later confirmed in analysis, as I will show through various vignettes. At this stage, I formed the hypothesis that Sara 'sucked' her mother's feelings of depression and guilt from a very early age. Sara's mother became 'dead' inside, and Sara herself stayed alive but experienced many difficulties.

Sara's mother also underwent several operations during Sara's childhood. Her uterus and thyroid gland were surgically removed after tumours were discovered on them. Sara always visited her mother in hospital, wrote her letters and tried to cheer her up. She perceived her mother as a 'fortress of strength'. The mother was secretive about her illnesses, and attempted to build a world in which nothing was amiss.

Sara was nineteen when her mother was hospitalised for the removal of a brain tumour. Seeing the scars on her scalp, the doctors enquired about her past, raising the possibility that she had been cruelly beaten on the head. They also hypothesised that these head scars might have been caused by the standard radiation treatment against lice which newcomers to Israel underwent. This procedure was discontinued when it was discovered to be a dangerous treatment which caused the appearance of growths in different parts of the body.

In order to illustrate the impact of Sara's unconscious fantasies about her mother's past on her own love-life and the need to concretise these fantasies through distorted, sado-masochistic relationships with men, I will describe Sara's first sexual relationship which was related to her mother's brain surgery. The working-through of this episode occurred when Sara was about one year into analysis.

Sara described her mother before the operation as 'thin, shaven, like the picture of a child in a concentration camp'. This time her mother was unable to hide her distress. Crying, she told Sara that she didn't know what would happen to her. She expressed the wish that Sara should have her rings and fur coat. Sara remembered how totally numb she felt, devoid of any feelings. There and then she decided she would lose her virginity. To that end she chose a male nurse who had taken intimate care of her mother prior to the operation. Sara hinted at her interest in having an affair with him. He took her to his home after one of her visits to the hospital, bragging about his relationships with women and telling her stories about his sexual relations with animals. Sara remembered that they had sex while his roommate was going in and out of the room. He afterwards sent her away without much ceremony. Years later, Sara saw his picture in the newspaper. He had become a dentist and was accused of sexually abusing his patients.

Telling me her story, Sara reacted to it sarcastically. 'What a good head I had!' she said with a laugh. 'A good head?', I wondered, 'it was your mother who had the head operation'. 'My head was totally separate from my body. I felt disconnected', Sara replied.

We attempted to understand this episode in light of the transference relationship. I was aware that I was being invited to be the sadistic analyst, who abuses Sara by breaking into her head (vagina) with his interpretations. At the same time, I had the task of removing a malignant growth (her fantasies about her mother's traumatic past) from her head in order to save her emotional life.

Sara described her narcissistic hurt, as well as her fragmented self and objects in the following way:

> When I am with people, I am always showing them my weak points; it is like I tell them – give it to me, hit me! On the other hand, I know that I am aggressive, critical of others. They have to accept what I am thinking. And I cannot be alone. It is insane, but I fill my void with men. I forget their names. I can only imagine I want an intimate relationship. I have only bits and pieces of experiences. Do you have any idea how it is not to be able to feel anything? I am totally disconnected from my feelings ...

Sara expressed her hope that through the analytic 'operation', her thoughts would become more connected to her feelings, and so help her become a better integrated person.

Working through the transference relationship enabled Sara to elaborate on her complex, painful feelings regarding this event. I will illustrate this by several excerpts from analysis: Sara described her experience of her mother's operation as a brutal rape. She continued by saying that she was unable to deal with her feelings of overwhelming pain arising from the possibility of her mother's death.

Gradually it became clear to me that in order for Sara to master these difficult feelings, she might herself have tried to become her mother. I realised that Sara's unconscious fantasy was that this would happen as a result of being touched by the same hands which took intimate care of Mother's body. Seeing the operation as rape (interchanging between the head and the vagina), Sara attempted to actualise it in a masochistic way upon her own body.

I would like to show through the following vignette that, similar to her mother's operation, Sara perceived the analytic 'operation' as rape, though also as a saving procedure.

With the occasion of 'The Day of Remembrance' in Israel, Sara saw the movie *Shoah*. In the session, she described a scene which had a great emotional impact upon her: the interview of a hair-dresser whose function it was in the camp to cut the hair of women before they went into the gas chamber. The man had a fixed smile all through the interview. When the interviewer finally referred to this smile, which was incongruous to the terrible things he spoke about, the man burst into tears, giving way to his unbearable pain. 'It was astonishing how he clutched at the

smile, so that the grief and the sadness would not come out', said
Sara.

I wondered if Sara wanted me to be like the interviewer who
broke the man's defences. Sara's answer to my unverbalised
question came through her further description of the movie. She
mentioned a scene in which appeared another survivor, a woman,
who underwent the Mengeles selection process. She was found
fit to work in the kitchens at Birkenau, and worked there twenty-
two hours a day. Sara added excitedly that when making his
decision, Mengele checked the woman's body with a stick.

After pausing for a while, Sara suddenly cried out: 'What am I
trying to tell you through this? I am afraid you will touch me. I
am like a soap bubble, and if you touch me I will burst.'

I was now aware of Sara's unconscious, conflictual wishes. She
wanted me to rape her, to break her defences, in order to save her
emotional life. At the same time she warned me that if I should
attempt to do so, it would bring about her destruction.

I didn't feel an interpretation would have been helpful at this
time to Sara, since she seemed to me to be so vulnerable. I
therefore continued to listen to her empathically, feeling this was
the only 'holding' (Winnicott, 1965) I could give her. Only much
later in the treatment was I able to make Sara aware of her unconscious, conflictual wishes towards analysis, and to help her work
them through (I illustrate this later in this chapter, with vignettes
from the fourth year of analysis).

Similarly to the analytic 'operation', the masochistic relationship with the male nurse also had a saving quality. Sara described
a book of stories which recently held her fascination, in which
beautiful blonde adolescents like her mother were saved by Nazi
lovers/tormentors. Referring to the male nurse as 'her Nazi
aggressor', she mentioned that she 'succumbed' to him. 'But, in
the end I stayed alive,' she said.

This confirmed my unspoken hypothesis that Sara wanted to
become Mother, the beautiful adolescent who survived. To this
end, she used the male nurse as a pawn for enacting a perverse
scene from her mother's imagined past, the purpose of which was
to save her own (her mother's) life.

Next session, Sara spoke in awe of her mother's strength and
astuteness. In comparison, she felt a failure: 'I don't think I could
have survived, I'm not as strong as she is, mother is a real survivor.'
In the transference, Sara bestowed upon me the qualities of the
'survivor' mother with whom she competed: 'I think you are

made of the same stock, if you want something nothing can stop you. I can never reach your professional status in my profession. If you had been through the Holocaust, you would probably have survived it.'

In response, I suggested to Sara that by 'succumbing to her Nazi aggressor', I felt she had enacted a drama in which she saved herself from an imagined danger and thus became a 'real survivor' like her mother, or me, in the transference.

Sara's reaction to my interpretation came through an episode of acting-out which followed this session. This episode revealed Sara's wish to save herself (her mother/myself) from the danger she exposed herself to, and in addition to that enabled us to discover and work through the underlying motives behind her need to become a saviour, namely the unconscious destructive wishes towards the maternal object.

After the session described above, Sara drove through a red light. At the same time, she noticed a young man waiting for the lights to change. She quickly made a U-turn, drew near and asked him, 'Are you free?' The man invited her to his place, and Sara followed without a word. Suddenly, becoming afraid and not understanding what she was doing there, she ran away.

My enquiry into this acting-out revealed Sara's wish to find a male partner and kick me out of her life, since she felt suffocated by me. But, at the same time, she put herself in what she imagined to be a dangerous situation, expecting the man she had approached on the street to rape, torture and kill her. At the last moment, she decided to rescue herself from the fantasised danger to which she had exposed herself.

Only after much psychic work had been done in the field of the elaboration of the relationship with Mother could Sara become aware, and work through, her intense anger in confronting Mother's death (experienced by a numbness in her feeling). It took a long time until Sara was able to acknowledge the existence of a certain wish that her mother should disappear and set her free. Sara recalled sitting at her ailing mother's bedside, when a 'crazy' thought crossed her mind: 'Now Mother is dying, a toast to life for me!'

The episode of deflowering described above, in which Sara sought a sado-masochistic relationship, and which was repeated in the transference, set the pattern for many of Sara's relationships throughout her life. Despite being young, beautiful and intelligent, and therefore having many opportunities, Sara seemed incapable of falling in love and forming stable emotional commitments. For Sara, being desired had life-saving implications. It meant saving herself as well as destroying the object, unconsciously perceived as her persecutor, a figure belonging to her mother's past.

At the start of a relationship, Sara usually felt a temporary enthusiasm for the desired sexual object, which imitated a state of falling in love. This was accompanied by sexual excitement, which temporarily heightened her illusion of being wanted. Soon, however, sexual fulfilment would arouse her need to vanquish her persecutor. This would coincide with the process of devaluing the consciously desired, but unconsciously hated object, resulting in the swift disappearance of both her excitement and her interest. The relationship usually ended with Sara 'discovering' that her partner was unable to withstand her anger, and his becoming weak and childish in her eyes. Sara often described the men as becoming sexually disinterested or even impotent.

The following are two examples of Sara's love relationships which illustrate her unconscious wish to become the phallic woman who destroys her persecutors by castrating them.

At the beginning of analysis, Sara described her current lover as a bright, handsome young man with a very promising career. The boyfriend had received an offer to continue his studies abroad, which he turned down in order to remain with Sara. This was concrete proof of his love and admiration for her, which heightened her self-esteem and made her feel wanted. Sara stressed the fact that her mother liked him for his ability to hold an intelligent conversation, his European manners and his refined taste with regard to the special coffees which she served. However, Sara's enthusiasm began to wane when he expressed his desire that they live together. Sara felt that she had absolutely no room for him in her apartment. She found a roommate for him, and he patiently waited for her for six months.

After that, they rented a little flat together, but the situation deteriorated. Sara felt stifled by his possessions, his books, his desk. She described herself with gusto as a witch with a broom in her hand, shouting at him, trying to move his things out of her way, while he cringed helplessly, hiding in a corner. Perceiving him as dependent upon her, Sara felt he was her victim and despised him for that. She now 'discovered' that he was cold and aloof, a loner. She complained that he lacked her ability to express emotions openly. Moreover, she felt that he was too weak and childish to provide the emotional support she needed. The boyfriend very quickly appeared to lose sexual interest in her, which led to many episodes in which he became totally impotent. Interpreting his impotence as revenge, Sara betrayed him with one of her former lovers and also considered abandoning him. The boyfriend, desperate to save the relationship, offered to marry her, thus expressing his unrealistic hope that stability would revive their dead love affair.

As in previous cases, Sara felt trapped and anxious, and wanted to get rid of the young man. She remembered with regret many of her previous partners whom she had abandoned who, in hindsight, seemed to have been much worthier of her love. Sara declined the offer of marriage, and shortly afterwards the boyfriend, vanquished, decided to move out of the flat. Sara was tremendously hurt by his 'abandonment' and 'mourned' his very belongings which she had been unable to accept from the beginning.

The second relationship also revolved around Sara's castration of her partner, in spite of the fact that this time Sara experienced herself as the man's victim. This relationship occurred during Sara's third year in analysis.

Her new lover was a man whom she had met years earlier during her army service. He was in the process of divorce, and had two young children. In the beginning, Sara appeared to be very happy with her lover's warmth and affection, and enthusiastic about their physical relationship. She was happy to give up one-night-stands, which usually left her feeling humiliated and abused. The love affair seemed to flourish until about the time of the man's divorce. By then, Sara had 'discovered' his 'mediocrity', feeling he was incapable of making a big success of his career.

Sara began demonstrating her anger through constant criticism and complaints. Whereas at the beginning of their relationship she had viewed the man as robust and athletic, she now felt he was too fat. She often nagged him about his table manners as well as about going on a diet, which he apparently refused to do. Sara described with disgust the way he drooled over his food, his enormous appetite, his lack of concern for how she felt about his appearance. She complained of being repelled by his body odour, which she attributed to poor personal hygiene. She felt there was no chance that her mother would like this man, as she did her former boyfriend who now seemed far superior.

Sara said her boyfriend reacted to her complaints by becoming taciturn and tried avoiding her anger by disappearing from her life for a couple of days after each painful incident. She was hurt by this reaction. She complained that she was being prevented from expressing her feelings openly. She considered him weak, childish, unable to withstand her anger. After a series of stormy outbursts, her boyfriend announced his decision to end the relationship.

Sara felt very hurt. She perceived herself as the victim of a man who had exploited her feelings and who had never really reciprocated her 'love' with the comfort and affection she so desperately needed.

I would like to illustrate the enactment of Sara's fantasies about Mother's traumatic past in the transference relationship. This episode occurred several months prior to the Gulf War, when there was already talk of a possible attack.

In her session, Sara described a movie she had recently seen, in which a famous German actor, Klaus Maria Brandauer, played the part of the Jewish protagonist. The plot revolved around a Jewish watchmaker who, in 1939, attempted to kill Hitler with a time-bomb but missed his target by seven minutes. He was sent to Dachau in 1945 and executed just before the liberation. 'Who was the little watchmaker who wanted to kill Hitler?', I asked Sara. 'Somebody who wished to change the face of history, to stop the brutality', she answered.

Sara arrived several minutes late for her next session.

S: It annoys me a lot to be late, I am always missing seven minutes.

I: Seven minutes? Do you remember your story from yesterday, about the destiny of the man who attempted to kill Hitler?

S: Yes, the watchmaker who attempted to kill Hitler and was seven minutes too late ... anyway we will be attacked, we are going to explode. Your office can be a wonderful sealed shelter. You can put all your family inside here.

I: I think you are telling me that you want to feel safe here in case of an external explosion. We are all afraid of that, you know ... but I have the feeling that you aren't just talking about explosions coming from outside, but also about you exploding from inside here with me in this room. Maybe you feel that I can be a good shelter for my family, but not really for you here in analysis ...

S: It is dangerous for me to touch my feelings, what will I do
      with my aggression and my envy? I don't think my feelings
      are legitimate.
I: Is it possible then, that by being late you are trying to avoid
      the 'explosion' of these feelings, and protect me from your
      wrath?

Sara responded to my question by missing her next session.
Thinking about her acting-out, I became aware that my interpretation could have been experienced by Sara as an empathic
failure. Was Sara's wrath directed only against me? Wasn't she
afraid that she would also 'explode' and that I wouldn't be a 'good
enough shelter' for her? Didn't Sara want me to defend her against
her own destructive aspects, the 'Hitler' inside her?

The session following the interruption began by Sara excitedly
describing another scene from the movie: 'A Nazi officer came into
the toilet and saw the protagonist, the poor watchmaker. Not
receiving the expected "Heil Hitler", he kicked the watchmaker
in the testicles and urinated on him.'

Following that, Sara described an incident at the school where
she worked. She made an appointment with some of the problematic children to help them with their problems, but instead
of doing her duty, she went to a lecture at the school which took
place at the same hour. Sara explained that she wanted to impress
the headmaster, who was supposed to be attending this lecture.
However, Sara felt ashamed and guilty for letting down and
abandoning the children who expected her.

Here, I referred to Sara's expectation and fear that I would
judge her behaviour, the fact that she had left the children
unattended. Maybe she felt, I added, that I would also criticise
her for not turning up for her session yesterday, reject her and
thus kick her painfully, like the Nazi officer from the film scene
she had described. But, I asked her, didn't she kick me away from
her by not turning up for analysis and by so doing, abandon the
problematic child in herself? Wasn't she her own Nazi aggressor?

This time Sara was better able to accept my interpretation and
began to reveal and work through her anger towards me, as well
as towards herself.

Working through the transference relationship facilitated further
understanding of her sado-masochistic relationships with men.

After each failure in her love life, Sara became very depressed
and expressed fantasies about children who were tortured, abused,

mutilated. These fantasies, which she tried to enact through her
sado-masochistic relationships with men, were connected to her
unconscious fantasies about her mother's experiences as a child
through the Holocaust. Much analytic work was required to
enable Sara to realise this, as I will show in my description of the
analysis further on.

It was only through my countertransference feelings during the
third year of our work together that I began to understand
something about Sara's sexuality which, until then, she had left
for me to guess at, namely, her intense homosexuality. This
homosexuality stemmed from her fixation on her damaged
mother and hindered her achieving an oedipal level and a stable
relationship with a man.

After each failure in her love-life, Sara perceived herself in the
transference as my unlovable child. How could an idealised
mother such as myself accept such a daughter – who was untidy,
unfeminine and who invariably failed to mature? 'I feel towards
you like towards my mother', said Sara. 'All my life she expected
something from me which I couldn't give.' Curiously enough,
Sara's frustration with herself aroused in me feelings of hopelessness and impotence in my role of analyst. I gradually realised
that while Sara had consciously bestowed upon me the role of
the omnipotent mother, she had unconsciously turned me into
her castrated lover.

Working through the transference relationship at this stage, Sara
became aware of her complex relationship with her internal
paternal image which I will not expand upon in this paper. I will
focus only on the role of the father as the protagonist in the drama
of the mother, and his introjection into Sara's self-image.

In contrast to her idealised mother, her father, when not totally
absent from the analytic discourse, was thoroughly detested by
Sara. She described him as disgusting, noisy, brutal and lacking
in refinement, thus giving an anal-sadistic quality to her portrait
of him. I pointed out to Sara that her intense rage against her
mother might actually have been directed against her father. We
then tried to work through Sara's conscious, as well as unconscious,
perception of her father. Consciously, she saw her father as the
agent responsible for her mother's unhappiness, unable to comfort
her mother and alleviate her depression. Unconsciously, she
assigned him the role of the Nazi persecutor who kept her mother
alive, but abused her sexually and tormented her psychologically. In her self-appraisal, Sara showed how closely she identified

with the anal-sadistic image she bestowed on her father, as well as with the castrated male lover she had turned him into. In her role as potential persecutor, she castrated her father's phallic capacities, thus turning him into a child. This subsequently became the pattern of her relationships with other men, as well as with me in the transference. In the role of her mother's inadequate lover, Sara felt castrated and impotent, like her father. In spite of her endless efforts, Sara felt incapable of lessening her mother's burden of depression and mourning. She projected this perception of herself as inadequate and helpless upon her male objects, as well as upon me in the transference, through massive projective identification.

The riddle of Sara's homosexuality was further elaborated upon in the transference through her description of a play she had seen abroad, entitled *M. Butterfly*. The play revolved around a complex homosexual love story. An English diplomat fell in love with a beautiful Chinese opera singer. The relationship which evolved lasted seventeen years, the sophisticated diplomat being 'blind' to the fact that his beautiful oriental concubine was a man. He was fooled by her disguise and perceived her as an innocent, modest woman, who refused to be seen naked, even though sexually she was most exciting.

Listening to Sara's story, I realised that she was warning me not to be blinded by her defences, but rather to be aware of who she really was beneath her disguise. Her long-term on-and-off relationship with a bisexual male, which I will now describe, shed light on her own bisexuality.

In this relationship, Sara felt that her boyfriend was sensitive to her needs, loving and unconditionally accepting of her. On the other hand, he was never faithful, and would bring home some of his homosexual boyfriends as well as another girlfriend. On the fantasy level, the relationship was often idealised, but in reality it was always on the verge of collapse. Sara left him when he offered to marry her, despising him for living on the fringe of society. In regard to him, Sara unconsciously played the role of the Aryan elite, while her boyfriend was assigned the role of the despised, good-for-nothing Jew. The roles were often reversed and he became the persecutor when, on several occasions, he threw her out of his house. Sara always came back to him when she wanted to get back at a current boyfriend whom she hated, or in between relationships. She found him soothing and warm, a source of the motherly affection she needed. On the other hand,

she was repelled by his masculinity. In the transference, in light
of a recent episode with this man which Sara vividly described,
we were both able to see her homosexual longing. After being
abandoned by her latest lover, Sara invited this boyfriend to
spend a weekend at her house. He obligingly came and spent the
evening reading in her office while she went to sleep alone. That
night Sara awoke, terrified by noises of someone roaming about
the house. Her immediate thought was that the rapist who often
threatened her in her fantasies was actually in her flat. She got
up in a panic, and looked terror-stricken at the 'stranger' who
laughed and said, 'You forgot that I was here in your house.' He
then took her in his arms, soothed her like a baby and put her
back to sleep.

Sara's story was accompanied by hysterical laughter, which to
me sounded like a painful sob. The sob became so strong and
uncontrollable that I was suddenly afraid. I felt that Sara was in
imminent danger of losing her sanity. In my countertransference,
I saw her as a child in agony, crying louder and louder, losing
control, tremendously threatened by fears of abuse and mutilation.
Gathering my strength, I told Sara that I felt she wanted me to
take her in my arms like a baby, and soothe what I heard to be
an uncontrollable cry of pain. She reacted to this by finally
calming down. Only after regaining control did she say, 'I realise
that I wanted to turn him into a woman. I hate his masculinity.
The next day, he wanted to sleep with me, and nagged me over
and over, like a child. I looked at him naked, and he appeared so
aggressive. A man seems like an animal to me. He eats a lot. I am
afraid of his erect member. I feel repelled by it.' Here, Sara
mentioned a story about an SS officer who wanted to rape a
twelve-year-old girl. The women around offered themselves to him
to distract him from the girl, but to no avail. The girl could not
be saved.

I asked Sara if she wanted me to save her from the fate of being
with a man. She answered: 'I've had fleeting thoughts about you
as my partner. It's a pity I can't marry you. I could live with you
for ever.'

Working through the transference relationship, especially her
homosexual longings, we discovered Sara's need to become the
battered, abused Holocaust child that her mother was in her
fantasies. Stuck in this role, Sara was unable to grow because she
could not go through the necessary mourning process related to
separating from her mother. She could not abandon the tortured

child of her fantasies and thus develop into a mature woman, capable of a normal love life.

I will illustrate this aspect of Sara's identification with the tortured child of her fantasies with some excerpts from the fourth year of analysis. Sara had recently read a paper on therapeutic work with children, which described the treatment of a little girl who became autistic after witnessing soldiers enter her house and kidnap her mother. The therapist saw her every day for five months but all of her interventions were to no avail. The therapist felt totally helpless and almost gave up. Then, suddenly, the child made a sound – the musical note 're'. Since the therapist herself was a musician, she heard the sound and reacted to it, a fact which helped the little girl begin talking to her.

I pointed out to Sara that by means of this story she was probably trying to convey how difficult it is for her to communicate with me and how much she would like to be understood by me on a non-verbal level, so that in the future she would be able to talk to me about things which she couldn't yet verbalise. Sara's reply revolved around the previous day's television programme, which dealt with a Holocaust survivor who went back to visit Auschwitz, where his maternal grandmother had died.

Following Sara's reply, I wondered aloud whether she saw herself as the little girl who had survived Auschwitz, the place where her maternal grandmother had perished. Is it possible, I asked her, that this was the music she wanted me to hear – the unspeakable sounds of the Holocaust, which belonged to her mother's childhood and which had become so much a part of herself?

The feeling that growing up and separating from her mother would mean leaving a dead mother behind (thus repeating her mother's fate) became clear during the next sessions. Sara told me a story she had heard from a friend about a little girl whose mother was selected by the Nazis for extermination. The girl was among the people who were allowed to survive and therefore remained in the camp. Someone noticed her terrible panic and pointed towards her mother, saying: 'Look, there's your mother!' The girl ran towards her mother who, instantaneously, knew how to react. She kicked the girl, denying any connection to her. The child remained behind and was saved. The mother went to her death with a terrible void in her heart. I asked Sara whether she felt that this story represented the story of her life. 'I have to fill the void', she replied. 'I will never be able to separate from

Mother. She once said that she lost her family. I am all the family she has.'

Further analytic work confirmed my hypothesis that in the transference I was the bereaved mother with whom the relationship was vital, but also lethal to Sara's growth and development. Sara was trapped by the unconscious fantasy that the life of the child meant the death of the mother. Over the course of several sessions, she described a film she had recently seen in which a child was caught by a sadistic adult, who suspended him upside down and proceeded to disembowel him (S = Sara, I = Ilany):

S: This is a terrible rape. All the torture. The child is on my mind all the time. Naked, with his belly-button out, blond, thin, hanging – without a rope. His screams of pain fill the air. Is he dead? No, maybe he's still alive. I wonder, are you putting these things into my head, or are you taking them out of it?

I: It seems that you are wondering whether I am your saviour or your torturer. But even if I were to remove these painful thoughts from your head, wouldn't it be like the sadist who took the child's guts out of his stomach? Last time you mentioned that the umbilical cord was the first thing to come out of his stomach.

S: Yes, the umbilical cord, my connection with Mother. Mother, who looks like a flower on the outside and keeps her pain inside. Mother, who ran through the woods with her sister and saw those corpses hanging from the trees. And it's funny, I see him again, this child, his belly-button out and sometimes dirt gets into it. The idea of putting my finger inside and cleaning my belly-button gives me the creeps. The child is in a void. I cannot touch my own belly-button.

Listening to Sara, I saw her as a child filling a void, while at the same time feeling that she was in a void. She had no firm ground under her feet, little reality in her life. I attempted to gently 'touch' the sore spot she was showing me, her belly-button. I, therefore, said to her:

I: I feel that you're telling me how sensitive the place we are touching is, the sore spot where you are connected to your mother.

S: I'm so tied to her, there's nothing to touch. I can never break away from her, never. If my mother dies, I'll fall apart.

Sara was quiet, and then continued:

S: This child that I see – naked, belly-button out, no face, when I come here and begin talking to you, I see him. He was born here. I had this dream of being pregnant, but not really pregnant; the foetus was clinging to me from the outside.

I asked Sara what came to mind when she thought of this dream. 'I don't know', she replied. 'It was so repulsive. I couldn't get it off me, like I can't get you off me.'

It then occurred to me that Sara experienced me in the trans- ference in the same way as she experienced her mother. Her mother was being like a child who clinged to Sara from the beginning of her life. On the other hand, I felt Sara was the foetus clinging to my body from the outside.

In my countertransference, I felt very sad, burdened by a heavy weight. The child whom we discovered here in analysis was not only tied to me by an umbilical cord, but from the wrong place, from the outside. She could never be born, be separated or ever grow up. Seeming to sense the heaviness in my heart, Sara added:

S: Sometimes, I wonder why you take such difficult things upon yourself, things connected with suffering, death, the Holocaust. I can't imagine holding myself together without you. I can never go away from here. Taking me on as a patient is really suicidal.

Again I felt that Sara was projecting upon me a feeling she may have experienced during her childhood, when she took upon herself her mother's suffering. Gathering my thoughts, I told her:

I: I think you are asking me why I take your suffering upon myself. Like the girl in your story about the Holocaust, you feel there is no way out. If I push you away from me towards life, you might fall apart emotionally. If I keep you with me, you are doomed to remain a battered child for ever. You see this as such a hopeless situation, that only a person who doesn't cherish his own life can fight for yours.

The working-through of our relationship helped Sara achieve some affective understanding:

S: It's strange, until recently I never considered my mother a victim of the Holocaust. I never thought about myself as having anything to do with her past. My mother seemed to be a strong woman, but she is a child after all. She was never close to me emotionally. Maybe that's why I myself became this child.

It was through the discovery of the battered child inside the mother that we obtained a shadow of the profile of the mature mother's absence. Behind the 'fortress of strength', Sara discovered a 'locked up' mother with whom she was never emotionally close, because her mother was always preoccupied with herself, unreachable without echo and sad beyond words.

At this point in analysis, searching desperately for something concrete about her mother's past, Sara visited her parents' house while they were away on holiday. She broke the lock on the cupboard where her mother kept some pictures of her parents and a diary in which she described her life through the Holocaust.

In analysis, we worked through Sara's aggressive act and her desperate need to fill the gap in her knowledge with a piece of her mother's history which had been missing.

First, Sara talked about the impact Grandmother's pictures had upon her: 'Grandmother, who looked so beautiful when she was just a few years younger, looked old when she was forty-four. It was as if the suffering of the world was imprinted on her face.' The sad look on Grandmother's face filled Sara with thoughts of the gruesome horrors she must have experienced before she died: 'Can you imagine how it must have been for a woman to send her daughters away and remain behind to die? How it must be to die alone?'

There was a short pause, then she added:

> I always held this fantasy about my grandparents going to the gas chamber. I wonder what it was like there. The chaos, the fear, the shouting ... what a nightmare! Some years ago, when we had to wear gas masks during the Gulf War, I thought I could give my mask to one of them ... but to whom? Who would I save and who would be doomed to suffocate? I felt it was like *Sophie's Choice*, impossible ...

During this period, Sara had a dream:

> In my dream, I entered an office building; it looked like an army office. The walls were painted yellow. It was a psychiatrist's office. I saw a desk and a cupboard which was open. Inside the cupboard was a transparent box. I could see flames inside the box. The fire was going to spread and I didn't know what to do. When the fire was extinguished, I took a rubbish

bag, a thin plastic bag, to collect the ashes. But the bag was full of wet rubbish. It was so heavy that I couldn't hold it. Then the rubbish was suddenly all over the place.

Associating to the dream, Sara said:

The cupboard which I saw in my dream was like the one in which I found Grandmother's pictures. It was Grandmother who went up in flames. The psychiatrist reminded me of a young man who works in the school, somebody I like. He wore shoes [Sara laughed] like the ones I saw you wearing during the winter. Mother has shoes like those too. I don't like those type of shoes. Do you know what we call them? 'Grandma's shoes'.

I asked Sara to tell me more of what came to mind when she thought of 'Grandma's shoes'. Sara recalled a childhood memory.

S: When I was a child my mother told me a fantastic story of how she received a postcard from her mother. When Grandmother travelled on a train she threw a postcard out of the window and it arrived at my mother's home. For many years, I believed that Grandmother was alive.

I: And what thoughts do you have about the wet rubbish?

S: Well, I thought that the wet rubbish symbolised live bodies, in contrast to the ashes. In my dream, I couldn't hold it any more, it spilled all over.

I: It seems to me that through your life, you had to keep the dead people, your mother's parents, alive. It must have been quite heavy for you, since you were not able to hold it any more. And I think you are looking at the flames from my office. Do you have any ideas why it looks like an army office?

S: Well, it probably has to do with the fact that nowadays we have an army, not like then ...

I: I think you are telling me, then, that you are now allowing yourself to look at your grandparents' death from a defended place, from analysis. And I believe that you want to 'assemble the ashes', to accept their death, in spite of the fact that you have kept them alive inside yourself for so many years.

It is only after we were able to work through Sara's mourning and guilt concerning the death of her grandparents, feelings which were probably unconsciously transmitted by her mother, that Sara was able to summon the courage to ask her mother questions about her Holocaust experiences. Like the unspeakable tones of the past, the tone of her mother's voice when answering Sara's questions made Sara weep with grief. She was no longer deaf to the sadness conveyed by her mother's depressed voice. Realising this, she had less of a need to act out this sadness in her own life.

Sara's enquiries into her past may have influenced her mother in deciding to make a trip to Poland, accompanied by her husband, to visit Auschwitz. Sara decided to join her parents on this trip. She felt that she had to take care of her mother, and not to leave her in her father's charge, since he was not young any more and she was afraid that it would be an emotional burden for him.

The enquiry into Sara's unconscious motives and wishes revealed that this trip was as important for Sara as it was for her mother. Sara wanted to face reality, to see with her own eyes the places where the flames of Auschwitz destroyed her grandparents.

On returning from her trip, Sara conveyed her impressions in a tone overwhelmed by emotion:

> A giant place, a tremendous parking place. Nobody gave you directions. Organised. There was a wall on which there were engraved all the names of people from Russia. There was some hope that Mother will find the names of her parents. Big pictures – lots, lots of pictures, you can go insane seeing the names and the pictures ... Mother looked for the names, she searched and searched. Tons of shoes, tons of hair, one cannot even imagine ... Mother was looking for something which may remind her of her parents, but there was nothing, nothing there, it was like her parents had been erased from this earth ...
>
> Afterwards we left Poland and travelled together by night-train. I had nightmares all night long. The small cabin, the noise, you have to tie yourself in a bed so you won't fall out. This reminded me of the Nazis. They came in all the time asking for the passport, the visa. I looked at the forests and thought about the dead people, dead bodies hanging from the trees ...

Shortly after returning from her trip, Sara expressed a tremendous need for love and sex. For some months, Sara had been involved in a very ambivalent relationship, which now was changing. It became intense and close as never before. Sara commented on a change in her emotional attitude towards this relationship.

> Something is happening to me, and this change frightens me.
> I have fantasies of staying with this man for life, and this is
> something I've never dared to think of before; a relationship
> was always like an abyss, a place into which I could fall and
> suffocate. And this man is not an easy person, he has his own
> problems. Will I be able to have a deep, long-standing rela-
> tionship like normal people have?

With the deepening of the relationship, Sara began to talk about
her strong urge to have a baby. She was almost forty-three and
felt that this was her last chance. She had doubts about her ability
to be a wife and a mother. If she was not able to stay with her
partner, would she be able to love this child? And maybe she would
do to the child what her mother did to her – destroy his capacity
to be a person of his own in the world?

Working through her fears and doubts, Sara, still very ambivalent,
decided for the first time in her life to give pregnancy a chance.
('Anyway, this cannot happen to me!', she remarked smilingly.)

After a couple of months Sara became pregnant and was terrified
by what she now called 'her irrational and irresponsible deed'.
Her first reaction was to accuse me of pushing her into doing
something she never really wanted to. Suddenly, all the tender
feelings which she had for her partner vanished, and she now found
him repulsive and totally unsuitable. In the transference, I became
the inadequate partner, a bad therapist, a conformist, who never
understood her real wishes and desires. Sara accused me of pushing
reality under her nose, making her aware of her biological age,
instead of being aware of her inner world. She accused herself of
lacking the strength needed to go her own way, to be different.
Her life up till now became idealised, while the future looked messy
and dark, almost catastrophic.

During this period I often felt hopeless and impotent in the face
of the tremendous anger which Sara directed against me. I had
doubts about the effectiveness of this analysis, in spite of the large
amount of work we had both invested in it for so many years.
Moreover, I began to feel guilty and asked myself questions, like:
Did I really cause her harm through analysis? Was she emotionally so immature that she could not become a woman and mother,
even though she probably also wanted this pregnancy? (If not,
she would never have let herself become pregnant.)

Sara's awareness, achieved through the analytic process, that
she was no longer a child was certainly painful for her. But could

she give up being a child following this realisation? Could she separate from her mother in order to grow up and mature?

An observation of Sara's non-verbal behaviour helped me to perceive the therapeutic relationship from a totally different angle. Every time Sara got up from the couch, she was looking intensely at me and left seeming somehow relieved. I had a strange feeling that Sara wanted to see if I could withstand her wrath, if I was still alive. When I made a remark about this peculiar behaviour, Sara said: 'Well, you see, I could never be angry with my mother. She was fragile, she could die if I hurt her.' This confirmed my hypothesis that Sara's anger was greatly due to her difficulty in separating from me. Like a true adolescent, she had to express her murderous rage towards me in order to be able to separate. The feeling that deep down Sara was grateful to me for surviving her wrath helped me to regain my belief in my analytic role, as well as in her analysis.

In spite of being so angry at her present situation, Sara still had no doubts whatsoever about continuing her pregnancy. At no point did she raise the possibility of an abortion. Slowly it came to light that, to Sara, having a child seemed like a miracle. Sara was not only antagonistic to the idea of having a child, she also had wishes to have one. An episode in which a friend of hers suffered a miscarriage showed that Sara was actually very frightened of losing her baby.

Sara's anger towards me was diminishing; she described the relationship with her boyfriend as having a totally different quality than any other relationship she had ever had in the past. This boyfriend loved her and tolerated her moods; she confessed she had warm feelings towards him. She appreciated him and considered him an adequate partner for her for life. Sara was now much more aware of her bouts of anger and criticism towards her boyfriend, and was usually able to control them better.

Gradually, I realised that the atmosphere in the sessions had become lighter. The couple decided to make their relationship public, a step towards marriage. Despite Sara's fears concerning such an announcement, they celebrated with a big party which she described to me in great detail. Apparently she even enjoyed it!

In this phase of analysis, we worked through her fears of the delivery as well as fears of losing her freedom by having a child. In spite of all this, Sara looked forward to being at home and happy at the prospect of taking care of her baby.

Sara asked for a couple of months break from analysis after the delivery, which I gladly agreed to. 'I am not going away yet', she warned me, 'I'll still be back ...'

In a recent session Sara mentioned to me: 'I think that over the last eighteen months I have reaped the fruits of the work we have done together throughout these years ...'

In spite of her difficulties, Sara felt that love and life were now possible for her. Like Sara, I also felt her interminable mourning was coming to an end.

Discussion

I would like to explore a central aspect of my thesis, that Sara's bereaved mother failed to mourn and, as a consequence, Sara could not mourn and so was unable to love.

For this purpose, I will address several critical questions: (1) Why should the inability to mourn entail the inability to love?; (2) Does a failure to mourn in the mother lead to a failure to mourn in the daughter and, if so, why?; and (3) Is there something in the mother's and, in turn, the daughter's, failure to mourn which is specific to Holocaust survivors? Can this process be seen in others?

1. In order to examine the impact of the inability to mourn on the capacity to love, I want first to differentiate between the 'normal' mourning, which accompanies the various phases of development, and the mourning connected to the traumatic loss of important objects. In this chapter, I express my assumption that there is a 'normal' mourning connected to growth and separation, which enables us to love.

Growth itself, the passage from one stage to another, involves the loss of certain attitudes, ways of life and relationships which, even though replaced by other, more developed ones, requires working-through mourning processes (Grinberg, 1964, 1992; Grinberg and Grinberg 1974). In cases where there is an impaired ability to go through the normal processes of mourning accompanying various life-stages, development and growth as an individual are impeded.

The capacity to love, which is part of growth, presupposes a normal symbiotic and separation-individuation phase (Bergmann, 1971; Bak, 1973). In order to form a love relationship, the child has to leave his parents behind and go through the 'normal' mourning which accompanies separation and growth. When there are difficulties in the process of separation, the mourning is avoided and the child remains attached to his parents, his capacity to form love relationships becoming impaired.

2. I want to continue by exploring the impact of the mother's inability to mourn on the daughter's capacity to mourn and, as a consequence, to love. We can view Sara's mother as a 'dead' mother (Green, 1986) who, because of her traumatic losses, was not able to be in touch with her feelings of mourning and guilt. These feelings, which, because of their devastating nature, could not have been contained in herself nor shared with an adult partner, had probably been projected onto her only daughter from very early childhood. The daughter introjected these feelings at a stage in life when the introjection–projection mechanism was dominant ('the milk which tasted like ashes'), experiencing her mother's traumatisation as if it was her own (Greenacre, 1967; Kogan, 1987, 1989a, 1991, 1993). Thus, the mother's pathological mourning (a mourning which was denied and therefore never resolved) became her own lot in life. The special relationship with the damaged mother hindered Sara from separating from her mother and from going through the 'normal' mourning necessary for forming a love relationship.

Sara experienced separation from the maternal object as lethal for her as well as for her mother. Therefore, although in her unconscious wishes Sara tried to get rid of her mother and bury her alive, she was also afraid that her grave would disappear like that of her relatives. Separation made living alone dreadful for Sara, as if she ran the risk of sinking into it, body and soul. On the other hand, as soon as she chose an object to occupy the place of her mother, she was threatened by her own hostile, aggressive feelings towards her, thus becoming her own mother and her emotional prisoner. In this way, Sara avoided separation and normal mourning. The increase in her manic defences became a powerful, integrated system directed against psychic reality and depressive experience (Klein, 1940). Sara's inability to love stemmed, therefore, not only from her ambivalence towards her love objects, as she had believed at the beginning of analysis, but also from the fact that her love was still mortgaged to her depressed, bereaved mother.

From another angle, it is also possible that Sara's mother's failure to mourn has deprived Sara of the opportunity to mourn the loss of loved objects, hindering her from achieving the ability to feel mourning, guilt and concern and thus contributing to the atrophy of her capacity to love (Josselyn, 1971).

3. Difficulties in the process of separation-individuation as a result of a pathological symbiosis and a special type of identification are characteristic to Holocaust survivors' offspring (Freyberg, 1980). The psychoanalytic literature about children of survivors describes the mechanisms employed in the transmission of the Holocaust to them as early, unconscious identifications which carry in their wake the parents' perception of an everlasting, life-threatening inner and outer reality (Axelrod *et al.*, 1978; Barocas and Barocas, 1973; Kestenberg, 1972; Klein, 1971; Laufer, 1973; Lipkowitz, 1973; Rakoff, 1966; Sonnenberg, 1974). The child feels compelled to experience the parents' suppressed themes, thereby echoing what exists in his parent's inner world (Laub and Auerhahn, 1984).

I find this identification with the parent similar to that which takes place in pathological mourning. Freud (1917) described this identification as a process in which the person in mourning attempts to possess the object by becoming the object itself, rather than bearing a resemblance to it. This occurs when the person renounces the object while preserving it in a cannibalistic manner (Grinberg and Grinberg 1974; Green, 1986). This process, which is typical of Holocaust survivors' offspring and which has been labelled 'primitive identification' (Freyberg, 1980; Grubrich-Simitis, 1984; Kogan, 1990, 1991) attempts to avoid the 'normal' mourning accompanying separation. In cases of children of Holocaust survivors which I have described elsewhere (Kogan, 1989a, 1989b) we can see the difficulty in forming a love relationship because of this inability to mourn separation from primary objects. As in the case of Sara, these children tend to avoid the mourning and pain incurred in separation by creating their parents' imagined traumatic experiences in their own lives, a phenomenon which was labelled 'concretisation' (Bergmann, 1982; Kogan, 1991, 1993) and which serves as a 'substitute for mourning' mechanism.

Sara also attempted to substitute for her mourning by living out her fantasies in a concrete form.

By attempting to stage the drama of her mother's past in the present, Sara not only ignored reality but also tried to substitute a new reality for it, as in psychosis (Freud, 1924). In this new reality, Sara's love objects acquired libidinal meaning only when they enabled her to play the role of the castrating woman or the

abandoned child of her fantasies. In both cases, she could act out
the drama of her mother's past by exposing herself to an imagined
danger and then saving herself through flight or promiscuity. Her
sado-masochistic relationships with men served as an important
defence against depression and mourning.

The transference relationship was also a stage upon which unconsciously expressed themes of survival and death connected to her
mother's past were acted out. Since Sara frequently felt that she
was in mortal danger, but was always ready to rescue herself (her
mother/myself), I often felt emotionally strained. The sense of
emergency created by the image of a constantly looming,
impending death aroused in me primordial feelings of distress
which I had to overcome before I could help Sara. The working-
through of my own feelings brought about further elaboration upon
the therapeutic relationship, facilitating affective understanding.
This eventually led Sara to better differentiation and lessened her
need to carry the burden of her mother's past (Klein and Kogan,
1986). Affective understanding also helped Sara become aware of
the unconscious meaning embedded in her actions, thus extri-
cating her further from her need for concretisation.

VII In the Same Boat[9]

(Psychoanalysis conducted during the Gulf War)

'Now war is in the crassest opposition to the psychical attitude imposed on us by the process of civilization, and for that reason we are bound to rebel against it; we simply cannot any longer put up with it.'

S. Freud (1932)

Introduction

According to Freud, 'cure' depends not only on freedom from symptoms, but also on the capacity to enter into intimate loving relationships and to be productive at work[10]. Thus, in order to effect a 'cure', patients in therapy must be brought to relinquish fixed patterns of thought, feeling and behaviour which might once have been adaptive but are limiting and self-defeating in current reality. Freud viewed insight as a major curative factor in psychoanalysis; that 'where id was, ego shall be' (Freud, 1915c, p. 275).

The debate on the curative effect of relational factors (the patient–therapist interaction) versus insight stems from an early controversy between Freud and Ferenczi. Freud carefully defined a neutral-interpretive approach, while Ferenczi (1920) advocated an 'active', caretaking approach, in which the analyst is emotionally available, warm and responsive. The nurturant-reconstructive and other aspects of Ferenczi's thought later found expression in the work of Alexander, Balint, Fromm-Reichmann, Guntrip, Khan, Kohut, Sechehay, Sullivan and Winnicott (Slipp, 1982).

I believe that during a time of existential threat, the curative effect of relational factors and of insight is different than during

133

peacetime. I would like to share some thoughts on performing psychoanalysis under such threatening circumstances.

Among the questions that Israeli analysts asked themselves during the recent Gulf War were: What are the feelings of people confronted with their own and their children's possible destruction? What is the significance of analytic treatment in such a situation? And what is the task of the analyst who finds himself in the same boat as his patient?

Both insight and relational factors are important in all analytic settings, but in my opinion, insight through interpretation should be postponed during times of existential threat while the relational factors that take place between analyst and patient during this period not only 'hold' the patient but may also lay the basis for improved analytic work once the threat has passed. This view should be seen in the context of Freud's statement that: 'In the confusion of wartime, in which we are caught up, relying as we must on one-sided information, standing too close to the changes which have already taken place or are beginning to, and without a glimmering of the future that is being shaped, we ourselves are at a loss as to the significance of the impressions which press in upon us and to the value of judgements which we form' (Freud, 1915c, p.275).

In this chapter I will illustrate the curative effect of insight and relational factors in the analyses of Holocaust survivors' offspring through the presentation of excerpts from the analyses of two patients seen before and during the Gulf War. Among other things, I will discuss how children of Holocaust survivors perceived reality during this period, the effect of present trauma on the memory of the past and how the strengthening of the ego forces becomes the focus of treatment during the war period.

The Case of Batia

I will first demonstrate how the use of increased insight helped to understand the unconscious meanings embedded in the actions of Batia, the daughter of Holocaust survivors, and how the further elaboration of this insight helped her relinquish the concretisation of fantasies connected to her mother's past.

Batia, a forty-year-old woman, married and a mother of three, is the oldest daughter of Holocaust survivor parents. Batia's mother and father both lost their families in Poland. The father joined a group of partisans who fought in the forests. The mother was about twelve years old when her parents and siblings were taken away by the Germans. She was saved by a Gentile woman who raised her as a Christian. At the age of sixteen she was sent to Germany on her way to Israel, where she met a man twenty-three years her senior, whom she married. A year after the marriage, at the age of eighteen, she gave birth to Batia. The family emigrated to Israel from Germany when Batia was one year old.

Batia described her mother as a childish person, who 'was never able to take care of herself or her children. She was very pretty, blonde and blue-eyed; but underneath she was always unkempt and dirty.'

Batia felt that she had been ambitious in school and was also ambitious in her career, as she considered success the only means for washing away the 'dirt' that she attributed to her origins. Striving for material achievement, she encouraged her husband to go into his own business, in which he was immensely successful. The couple built a luxurious house in the suburbs, but when they moved into it Batia became depressed. She hated its beauty and elegance, and could not explain her unhappiness to herself or anyone else. Below is an excerpt from a session dealing with Batia's present quest for another, better house, which is related to her unconscious attempt to recreate her mother's past in her own life. This episode occurred about nine months before the Gulf War (B = Batia; I = Ilany):

B: Over the past ten–fifteen years, all I dreamt about all day long was owning a house. I wanted a house of my own; that would be the fulfilment of my ambitions. A house is also a status symbol, perhaps indicating a certain lifestyle. I wanted to live in a house like you see in those pictures in magazines. The problem with the house my husband and I built is that the surroundings aren't like those in my dreams. There's no green forest, no lake. I have to move. It is definitely in the wrong location. And when I leave it, I won't sell it but I'll turn it into a monument. The house will show everybody what we've been able to achieve.

I: Why do you want to make a monument out of your house?

B: I'll tell you why. It's connected to my wanting to go to Poland. I want to cut out a yellow star and say to them – Look at me, with my yellow star and my Israeli flag. I'm back! You didn't succeeded in destroying me. I'm proud of what I am,

I'm no longer ashamed even though for many years I was ashamed.

I: It must be difficult for you, with your pride, to show me all the things you've been ashamed of.

B: Yes ... I'm a complex person. Yesterday I saw one of our cabinet ministers on TV. He was so vulgar, repulsive, illiterate. This government of ours – they're all stupid. It's only when I go to concerts that I see the refined side of Israel.

I: I think you're telling me how you feel about yourself – you have a refined aspect but you also have an aspect which you consider vulgar and stupid.

B: Well, you know, the houses here are dirty. There isn't much aesthetics here. I personally don't leave the house without nail polish on my fingernails and toes. My underwear is always very clean. My mother's dirty, you know. Her bra and panties are dirty. Mother's oven is dirty, her bathtub is dirty.

I: It seems that you have to show a refined, clean aspect on the outside in order to cover what you consider the vulgar, dirty places inside you.

B: Mother is a lady on the outside, but far from one on the inside. She used to say all the time that she was a Christian. But she was a liar. And in spite of all her show, she was never interested in anybody but herself. That's dirty.

I: You seem to have many doubts about my feelings towards you, whether they are real or fake.

B: You're clever. This is a game you're playing. You're playing the role of doctor. Mother didn't even try to fake a role.

In the countertransference, I felt rejected while at the same time sensing Batia's neediness.

I: I feel that you're trying to keep me at a distance, while at the same time you are feeling lonely and sad.

B: I am very sad, that's true. I want to hide my sadness, but then I feel that I'm playing games. I'm ashamed to tell you that lately I haven't showered every day. I feel dirty. I wish I could take my house and move it to another place. I need land around me, quiet, trees, a lake.

I: Is it possible that you're showing me the sad, 'dirty' part of yourself, hoping that I'll take you to another place inside you, where you'll like yourself better?

B: You're right about that, I don't like myself very much ... You know ... when I was younger, I read a lot. I even copied descriptions of landscapes into a notebook. I loved it so. I read about a house where one hundred Jewish children were saved. Now, everything is sinking back into history. I have a need for this house.

We sat quietly for several moments. I was aware of Batia's longing for an emotional home in analysis, a yearning which I very well knew she couldn't afford to acknowledge at this stage. I was overwhelmed by a feeling of frustration, and I had the fleeting thought that I would never be able to reach this woman, that it was like wanting to reach somebody living in another era, something unrealisable ...

I: What you seem to be sharing with me today is your sense of loss and intense longing for something which can never be fulfilled ... Tell me more about the book from which you copied out descriptions ...

B: I don't remember ... I think ... it comes back now ... The name of the book is *My Hundred Children*. It's about a house in Zakopane, Poland, where children were saved from the Nazis. The land surrounding the house was beautiful. It had large grounds, a forest, a lake. (Looking perplexed) Is it possible that this is the house I'm looking for – like I'm trying to become my own mother and live her life in the present?

This vignette illustrates how Batia became aware of her wish to exist on two levels of reality. During this session she conveyed to me, through projective identification, her futile attempt to live both in the present and the past. I did not immediately make a direct transference interpretation. Instead, my interpretation above was based on the resonance of this affect in me – the feeling that I couldn't even reach her. As a result of this interpretation, Batia felt understood enough to be able to search for and find that aspect of her internal world that she was attempting to externalise.

We were now able to work through Batia's feelings of being 'dirty'. Batia connected these feelings to the story of her mother being saved by a Gentile woman in whose 'dirty' house she had lived. In spite of viewing her mother's attempt to be considered Christian as 'dirty', Batia also accused her of being a 'dirty' Jewess. She hated her mother for being a dirty Jewess under her Aryan façade, and at the same time felt that she herself was one. Though massively denied, the fantasy of her mother behaving 'dirty' – being

sexually promiscuous in order to save her life – now surfaced.
Further analytic elaboration of this insight provided a framework
in which Batia's newly acquired knowledge of herself facilitated
differentiation from her mother's past.

I will now illustrate how I attempted to deal with Batia's feelings
of rage, impotence and terror immediately after the outbreak of
the Gulf War. The generally accepted procedure in psychoanalysis,
that of interpretation, no longer seemed appropriate, as will be
explained later; other factors pertaining to my real relationship
with the patient came to the fore and took precedence over it.

B: (smiling) Today I heard the words 'mass destruction' all day
     long. They ran through my head all the time. I have no idea
     if a sealed shelter is enough protection against chemical
     warfare. Is it?

I was aware that in the transference Batia was asking whether I
was capable of sheltering and protecting her against the terrible
things which might happen. But, feeling that such a transference
interpretation would place me in an omnipotent role, I related
instead to the affect accompanying her words, by trying to
understand her inadequate smile.

I: I wonder ... you were smiling all the time.
B: I'm crying underneath. I'm afraid of a gas attack. In the film
     Shoah, there was this scene of people going to the gas
     chambers. They were naked, urinating, defecating – when
     you're afraid, it comes out of you. When I go to the sealed
     room, I have to go to the toilet. The thought that comes into
     my head is that I hate the Germans. I've always both hated
     and admired them. But now, the dirt is coming out again with
     their chemical warfare. I'm afraid that gas will enter my gas
     mask. I become terribly anxious. I think that maybe I'll send
     the children to the US. When I sit there with the gas mask
     on my face, I feel ashamed for my children; that I brought
     them into a world where we have to wear gas masks. They
     sense my anxiety. It's transmitted through the air. There's
     catastrophe on the horizon. I'm like a watchdog. I can smell
     where danger is coming from and I have healthy senses. I don't
     want to repeat my parents' experiences.

I was aware that, in the transference, Batia was expressing her
doubts about my ability to prevent a catastrophe. Again, I had
the feeling that a transference interpretation at this point would

place me in an unrealistic role. Since I knew that Batia and I were really in the same boat, I expressed my own feelings: 'We are all threatened by death and destruction ... we all want to live.'

Batia reacted by referring to a real event which I too had recently seen on television; something which put terror into the hearts of all Israelis. 'Yesterday, I saw a little girl on TV whose house had been bombed. She wanted to go home, but couldn't because her house had suddenly become a pile of rubble.'

Once more, in the transference, I was aware that Batia was afraid that I, in my role of her emotional home in analysis, would be destroyed. But this was not a mere fantasy coming from her internal reality. Right then, it was a very feasible possibility. I could therefore only acknowledge our common feelings of terror when confronted with possible destruction. However, I did point out to Batia that her fear that her house might be turned into a pile of rubble had a special meaning for her, because it was connected to a possible repetition of her mother's past in Batia's own present reality. Batia, who throughout her life had so desperately sought her mother's house which had been destroyed, was now confronted with the possibility of a similar catastrophe in her own life. Only later on in analysis could we deal with Batia's transference feelings concerning the possibility of my destruction.

The Case of Hannah

The following clinical vignette, which occurred five years before the Gulf War, illustrates a patient's attempt to understand her need for concretisation through the interpretation of the role she assigned to the therapist in the transference and the roles which she acted out.

Hannah is the daughter of a Holocaust survivor whose first wife perished in the Holocaust, and who spent much of the war in hiding.

During the first year of analysis, when Hannah was thirty-two years old and single, there were many episodes of concretisation which expressed her unconscious attempt to re-create the fate of her father's first wife. The fact that she was living in Israel, surrounded by Arab animosity, was very much connected to her fantasies about her father's past.

Hannah rushed back to analysis from a trip to Europe in a state of panic and tremendous anxiety to relate that she was in great danger because 'an Arab is after me'.

It turned out that Hannah had met an elegantly dressed man in the lobby of her hotel who appeared to her to be an Arab spy. Despite her foreign citizenship and the fact that she had been living in Israel for only a few months, she immediately told him that she was an Israeli citizen. After going to dinner and a film with him, Hannah went to his room, where the two had sex without uttering a single word. Suddenly Hannah realised that she didn't even know his name. Panic-stricken, she immediately made up an excuse that she had to go to the toilet, dressed hurriedly, grabbed her handbag and left the room. Two hours later she was on a plane to Israel.

Back in Israel, she informed the hotel that she had left a pair of shoes there and gave them her address so that they could be forwarded to her. Immediately after this, she desperately came looking for me, convinced that the 'Arab spy' would now pursue her.

Hannah connected this episode to the film *The Night Porter*, which she had seen many years before on a trip to Europe. As she related it, the film was about an encounter (several years after the concentration camps were liberated) between a Jewish woman who had spent her adolescence in a concentration camp and the Nazi officer in that camp who had been her tormentor. In this encounter, the past prevailed over the present, and the protagonists, propelled by a force greater than themselves, resumed their concentration camp roles of persecutor/victim. The man sexually abused the woman, and then, no longer able to return to reality, killed her.

In attempting to understand Hannah's need to act out her unconscious wishes and fantasies connected to her father's first wife, I pointed out that she was assigning me the role of her saviour, while attempting to bring this woman back to life by becoming her. But, I added, she was trying to kill the woman by placing herself in danger of being killed by the Arab/Nazi. Following this interpretation, Hannah supplied more material which showed that behind her wish to be the victim lay her unconscious wish to become my persecutor. Over the course of the five years of analysis, we worked through, among other things, the special bond existing between Hannah and her father which made her re-create his past in her own life. We elaborated upon her feelings of mourning and guilt, which had been transmitted to her in non-verbal ways through the particular atmosphere which prevailed in her home. All of this enabled Hannah to separate from the burden of the past and build a life of her own.

Five years after she began analysis, during the Gulf War, Hannah was already married and the mother of two. The vignette presented below took place four weeks into the Gulf War, during which time Hannah had not come to analysis. (This was quite uncommon, because a few days after the war began almost everyone went back to work during daylight hours, and most patients returned to treatment.) Through this fragment from analysis we can see Hannah struggling for the increased insight that would allow her to disentangle her fantasies about the Holocaust from the traumatic events taking place in current reality (H = Hannah; I = Ilany):

H: The first night I heard the siren, I was panicky, shaking all over, I couldn't breathe. My husband wasn't home, he was in the army reserve. Dani (her one-year-old) was screaming, with his face squashed against the plastic anti-gas tent. It came to me that any minute we might all be gone, the children as well. Did you feel this way, too?

I: Are you asking if you had the right to feel this way? The first night was a scary experience. Gas masks on our faces for three-and-a-half hours, without knowing what might happen, to be threatened with destruction ...

H: I was ashamed of how scared I was. It took me some time to come back to analysis. But, now, it's like a routine. You can get used to almost anything. That Scud attack was on a Friday night. I was alone with the two babies, I wasn't wearing my contact lenses and I couldn't see through the mask. Ben [her husband] wasn't home, and the babies were both hysterical. Haim [the older child] wanted a bottle. But they said that we shouldn't take off our gas masks, so I couldn't give him one ... I know it was pretty good that I could go through all this without needing to talk to you.

I: Now that you're stronger, you're telling me about the baby aspect in yourself, which needed my tending and care. But you were probably afraid to 'take out' this aspect and be in touch with it.

H: That's true. I felt I had to be strong, that I couldn't allow myself to be a baby, now that the children were relying on me. But there's something very important I wanted to tell you. For so many years I've been preoccupied with thoughts of the

Holocaust. I feel that now it's not like it was then. Now we have our own country ... army, government. Even if anything chemical falls here – everyone made the connection with Germany – I don't feel that we're on the verge of another Holocaust.

I: You're struggling to disconnect the present from the past.

H: Ben thought we should go abroad, or to Jerusalem. But I said no. My fate and the children's is linked to the fate of this country. Somewhere deep within me I knew that I was sitting comfortably in my house, with my children listening to the news on Israeli Army Radio Station. That didn't happen in the Second World War. I'm not comparing the two experiences, but contrasting them instead. We have food, our house is heated. The only thing that you have to overcome is your fear. It's the fear of the unknown. The first night we didn't know what to expect. Now it's different. I talked with my father yesterday. He said the Jews have been through worse.

One day after the war ended, Hannah had a session.

H: It's nice to be without gas masks. But it happened so quickly. Maybe we should have kept them a little longer, until they're absolutely sure. So now psychologists can study Israel in the aftermath of the war and gas masks.

I: You mean that now that there's no longer any danger, you don't feel I'm as close to you as before? That I've become the remote psychologist who might be interested in your reactions for research purposes.

H: I mean that there will be effects, that life cannot go back to normal. Thursday, when I opened up the sealed room, I felt like calling and asking for an additional session on Friday. I was in a daze. I was crying. You have to hold yourself together, but afterwards ... The day after the first Scud missile, I was in the garden with the children. I thought about my father who hid in a cellar for months during the war, and couldn't see the sun. Now he often lies in the garden. He likes the sun, his family around him, safe and sound. I like being in the garden, like my father. Now I have the feeling that I have to go places. You start appreciating things more. I took the children to a kibbutz, to a playground. Just being free is amazing. This weekend I want to go to Jerusalem, I want to take some trips.

I: Then, to come back to analysis, to bring the child aspect in you to this playground is to come back to life and freedom. You want to continue the trips inside yourself.

H: I used to want to be home with the children. Now, I'm sick of being home. I want the children to see the country. Everyone has the feeling of coming out of hiding.

I: You hid at home for four weeks before you decided to come back to treatment.

H: I know that Father was in hiding during the war ... after he left to look for food, when he came home, his wife and children were gone. This may be the reason why I couldn't leave the house for a whole month, although I saw others around me working and living as usual.

I: You seem to be comparing the present situation to your father's past experiences.

H: It's very different, because it didn't touch us. Let's say that we were threatened by someone like Hitler; for most of us it was just a threat. And it affects you as much as you let it. Sometimes I felt like telling you – this is nothing, it's just a threat. But the next day, I was so anxious, I didn't send my child to nursery school.

I: You had to be strong and mature, you wished to calm me and yourself, but inside you were anxious and couldn't send the little girl in you to analysis. You had to seal her in a room inside yourself. Now we can open up this place and be more in touch with what's there.

H: I could have left. I was alone, my husband wasn't home. They said a lot of Israelis were leaving ... I couldn't go. If I went abroad, I would be preoccupied with what's going on here ... People there would be going about their lives. The only people I feel close to are those who reached out to me here during recent years. The terrible thing was the threat to the children. Then why didn't I take them abroad? Because I couldn't, that's all.

I: What you seem to be hinting at is that one of the reasons you didn't go abroad was because you knew that I was here, reaching out to the threatened child inside you.

H: You called me immediately after the war broke out and asked me if everything was alright. That was a very personal thing to do.

From these sessions, we can see Hannah's resistance to her regressive urges for shelter and protection at the beginning of the Gulf War, when she didn't allow herself to come to analysis. Now, at the end of the war, through my interpretations, Hannah became aware of her fear of being in touch with her infantile longings, which threatened her mature functioning during the stressful period of the Gulf War. Through increased insight, she came to understand that she had been feeling and behaving like her father, who had been in hiding during the Holocaust and lost his family when he left home for a short while. Feeling stronger and better able to cope with reality, Hannah could continue her struggle to disentangle the present reality from her father's horrendous past.

Discussion and Conclusions

I shall now discuss, first, the curative effect of insight and interpretation in the analyses of Holocaust survivors' offspring, and, second, the curative effect of the patient–analyst relationship during a period of existential threat. It is my belief that insight, facilitated by the therapist's interpretations, plays an important curative role in the analyses of children of Holocaust survivors. These interpretations become a primary tool in attributing meaning to the patients' acting-out and in helping these patients translate the acting-out into cognitive and verbal modes. Through heightened insight, the patients become aware that their symbolic, displaced actions are unconsciously addressed to lost loved ones. This leads them to the realisation that they are in effect living on two levels: their own present and the fantasy world connected to their parents' traumatic past. Elaborating these insights in the context of the transference relationship eventually leads the patients to a better ability to differentiate between their present life and their parents' past.

To assess the curative effect of insight and relational factors during the Gulf War, I shall first examine the way in which the offspring of Holocaust survivors perceived reality during this period. This includes such questions as how present trauma affects the memory of the past. There is no time in the unconscious (Freud, 1915a), only the articulation of meanings (Schaeffer, 1980). Past and present merge in the unconscious, so that the meanings that were, still are, and the meanings that are, affect and change those that were (Loftus and Loftus, 1980). Moses (1993b) stressed the unconscious component found particularly in Holocaust survivors who fear a repetition of the past they have lived through, even though this is not realistic.

The psychoanalytic model of trauma is composed of two events: a later event that causes the revivification of an original event, which only then becomes traumatic (Laplanche and Pontalis, 1967). For the children of Holocaust survivors, the experience of the Gulf War reactivated the trauma of their parents' past. And, becoming linked to past horrors, these Gulf War experiences took on the quality of childhood fears and nightmares. This threatened to destroy the boundary between inside and outside, between reality and fantasy (Auerhahn and Prelinger, 1983). Many such offspring perceived the missile attacks on Israel as the harbinger of another Holocaust, which they had always anticipated with terror. Israel's policy of non-retaliation only reinforced this feeling and brought back the fear of again becoming 'sheep led to the slaughter', of being unable to avoid repeating the fate of their parents. The involvement of German companies in the development of Iraq's chemical weapons, especially gas, brought the nightmare of the past even closer to the present. In other words, for the children of Holocaust survivors, the present terror was the frightening realisation of fantasies of a traumatic past.

There is no simple answer to the question of whether this connection of the past to the present was specific only to 'the second generation' of Holocaust survivors. A large segment of the Israeli population linked the threat of the Gulf War with the Holocaust history of the Jewish people. It is therefore possible that the collective memory of past traumas, in a certain sense, turned us all into a 'second generation'.

Some thoughts occurred to me regarding the similarity between Saddam Hussein's ideology during the Gulf War and the Nazi ideology which was analysed by Chasseguet-Smirgel (1989) in her paper 'Some reflections of a psychoanalyst on the Nazi biocracy and genocide'. Basing her hypothesis on 'The archaic matrix of the Oedipus Complex' (Chasseguet-Smirgel, 1986), the author claimed that the body of the German people, the Aryans, in order to become one with the body of the Mother – the German homeland – had to remove all obstacles which were preventing this union (the Jews). In the same manner, Saddam Hussein declared his wish to cleanse the Holy Land of the 'American-Zionist Jews' (his label for the Israeli people), so that the unification of the Palestinian people with their Motherland could take place. We can see this as Saddam Hussein's identification with his Palestinian brethren's returning to a unified Islamic world. I wondered whether this was why Saddam Hussein named this war the 'Mother of Wars'?

To resume the exploration of transference and countertransference as well as of the psychoanalytic technique during the war, I would like to point out that the generally accepted procedure in psychoanalysis – that of interpretation – was not always valid. For analysts were no longer observers who, by training and circumstances, are 'not supposed to' react personally to their patients' internal crises or external conditions. As early as 1937, Glover wrote: 'It seems that we must credit therapeutic effects ... not solely to interpretation, but to interpretation in confrontation with other factors ... namely, to the humane relation in the transference' (Glover *et al.*, 1937). Thus, during the Gulf War, analysts mostly 'maintain[ed] and support[ed] the patient' (Spitz, 1956), and conveyed a feeling of togetherness by acknowledging their own feelings in the face of possible destruction, rather than serving as a blank screen.

During this period, the aim of treatment with the offspring of Holocaust survivors was to help them perceive the reality of what was happening to them at the time, rather than concentrate on what they imagined had happened to their parents in the past. Since coping with current reality, as threatening as that might be, is different from dealing with patients' feelings about their parents' past, which they can neither influence nor undo, it seemed necessary for me as an analyst to reinstate my patients well and truly in the present reality. I did this by giving them evidence of my own feelings as a person who was sharing the same reality, without letting myself be paralysed by the rule of neutrality (Nacht, 1962).

What I have attempted to describe here as specific to analysis during this period, and especially to the analysis of Holocaust survivors' offspring, took place mainly in the realm of the 'real relationship' between analyst and patient. Measured against the total length of analysis, this phase was comparatively short. Nevertheless, this phase of analysis during the Gulf War, in which there was an existential threat to both analyst and patient, was characterised by a special relationship which enhanced subsequent analytic work. The patient perceived the analyst as placing external reality in the present, by sharing his own emotional reaction to it with the patient and thus not blurring the boundaries between now and then, as their parents had done. From this point of view, this phase was similar to what Grubrich-Simitis (1984) called 'the joint acceptance of the Holocaust reality'.

During the war, like many other analysts, I came up against greater resistance to regressive urges for shelter and protection in my patients. I was confronted with the dilemma of how to modify the analytical technique so that it would be effective in a life-threatening situation. For the course of recovery, based on strengthening the ego, is brought about by the progressive acquisition of insight. But the analytical situation causes regression, and this weakens the ego so that it becomes increasingly susceptible to fear – which in turn weakens it even further. Moreover, people who suffer from blurred ego-boundaries, like the children of Holocaust survivors, experience insight into their infantile longings as even more threatening to their ability to cope than do others.

It is my experience that the analyst must respect this resistance and support the ego until these patients feel safe enough to discover and work through their childish aspects. As illustrated in the vignettes which I have presented, I reacted to my patients' plight during the war by talking naturally about our common experience, dealing with their preoccupations and worries on a realistic rather than a fantasy level. I did, however, point out their concealed terror in connection with the Holocaust past of their parents.

Only towards the end of the war, when patients felt more secure because of better stabilised ego boundaries, did I attempt to interpret their regressive transferences. Since they were then better able to cope with the anxiety-provoking reality, it was possible to use increased insight to work through their infantile longings which had been evoked by the actual trauma, and their resistance which had appeared with the outbreak of war. When successful, this process enabled the patients to rely on me, and eventually upon themselves, in dealing with the tensions and anxiety aroused by the frightening reality.

I discovered that the relational factors during the war often strengthened the patients' mental organisation to the point where they could dissociate some of the feelings of anxiety and pain caused by the real threat they were facing from those linked to fantasies about their parents' past. This eventually facilitated a better ability to cope and, in many cases, improved subsequent analytic work.

Epilogue

I did not manage to save
a single life
I did not know how to stop
a single bullet
and I wander around cemeteries
which are not there
I look for words
which are not there
I run
to help where no one called
to rescue after the event
                                    J. Fickowski (1981)

This book is based on my clinical experience, through which I became aware of the extent to which the complex patterns of unconscious thoughts, feelings, expectations, anxieties and defences, which my patients brought into the analytic situation, were coloured by the imagery of the Holocaust. This was communicated to me through the patients' use of words as well as through their actions, which contained unconscious symbolic meanings from their parents' past. The transference relationship often became a stage upon which unconsciously expressed themes of survival and death were acted out. The patients were the protagonists in their parents' drama, alternately playing the roles of victims/persecutors and assigning complementary roles to me. Thus, the transference was not only 'full of meaning and history' (Joseph, 1989) from their own lives, but also full of the meanings and history of their parents' traumatic past. It was through my observations in the immediate transference relationship of my patients' need to live out their parents' past that I realised the profound psychic impact of the parents' massive traumatisation on the sense of self and reality of their offspring.

In my work with second-generation patients, I became fascinated with two central themes. The first is the interplay between fantasy and reality in their lives. Because their minds were permeated with traces of their parents' experiences, they lived in a double reality – their own and that of their parents. The second is the patients' struggle to construct a new, separate and more cohesive self by means of the therapeutic relationship. I felt that psychoanalysis could help my patients mend the damage their ego had inflicted upon them in fantasy and make them conscious of what it was that compelled them to act out their fantasies, thus helping them achieve a life of their own. This book illustrates these two central themes, which occur again and again in the analytic material.

In order to better understand the complex interplay between fantasy and reality in these children's lives, I wish to examine two processes which lie at its core: first, the transmission of trauma from one generation to the next; and second, the need for 'concretisation' (Bergmann, 1982; Kogan, 1987, 1989a, 1989b, 1990, 1991, 1993, 1995) – the compelling unconscious need to recreate and relive the parents' traumatic experiences and their accompanying affects in their own lives, as if these were their own story.

I will first provide a brief explanation of these processes. I will then show how they apply to the analytic process against the backdrop of the case studies described in the book.

The Interplay between Fantasy and Reality in Offspring of Holocaust Survivors

Process I – The transmission of trauma

Ever since Freud abandoned his theory which attributed the cause of hysteria to real events, psychoanalysis has emphasised the ego's response to what was done to it in reality as well as in fantasy. For the offspring of Holocaust survivors, the trauma which was transmitted to them is found in a realm between fantasy and reality. The reality of the trauma belongs to the parent's life experience; however, by means of his imagination the offspring attributes it to himself. This transmitted trauma is a fantasised sharing of the real trauma (Oliner, 1982; Kogan, 1989a). The fantasy is nourished by the offspring's perception of the often unspoken reality of the trauma that the parents suffered and the anxieties it generated.

The perception of the parent's traumatic experience occurs during very early stages of the child's development. The child experiences the severe trauma (either an acute occurrence or a chronic state) of his mother or others close to him as though happening to his own self, if he is at a stage or in a state where the introjection–projection mechanism is dominant (Greenacre, 1967).

In the analyses described in this book, the transmission of the trauma to the offspring did not necessarily occur as a result of situations in which the parent was traumatised while the child could observe it, but rather occurred as a result of situations where the parent carried within himself the undigested memory of past severe traumatisation.

The psychoanalytic literature regarding children of survivors describes the mechanism employed in the transmission of the Holocaust to them as early, unconscious identifications which carry in their wake the parents' perception of an everlasting, life-threatening inner and outer reality (Axelrod *et al.*, 1978; Barocas and Barocas, 1973; Kestenberg, 1972; Klein, 1971; Laufer, 1973; Lipkowitz, 1973; Rakoff, 1966; Sonnenberg, 1974). The child feels compelled to experience the parent's suppressed themes, thereby echoing what exists in his parent's inner world (Laub and Auerhahn, 1984). Krell (1979) points out that children of survivors are themselves survivors of a sort, as 'by all odds, neither the parent, nor the child were to exist'.

Levine (1982) suggests that trauma can be transmitted to the children of survivors in three ways: first, through the impact of the Holocaust trauma on the parenting capacities of the child; second, through the child's identification with, or rejection of, certain traits in his parents that can be linked with their Holocaust experiences; and third, through the child's phase-specific elaborations of his parents' experiences. He notes three areas which he considers to be particularly problematic: (a) conflicts around the development of autonomy, the development of self-object differentiation, and identity formation; (b) problems with guilt, aggression and super-ego development; and (c) impaired reality-testing, which he views as a 'localized failure to appreciate the make-believe character of fantasy' – a theoretical understanding which is akin to the concept of concretisation which I explore further on. In a similar vein, Phillips (1978) points out that children of survivors hesitate to express negative affects for fear of overwhelming or alienating their parents. As a result, they repress their anger and their 'unconscious fantasies of aggression towards [their] parents hypertrophy so intensely that these begin to approximate the real, horrifying experiences of torture and extermination that [their] parents experienced at the hands of the Nazis'.

In this book I explore and illustrate these early identifications from the point of view of the transference relationship. The powerful process of fusion in the transference, the patient not being able to differentiate between himself and me, often left a powerful impression upon me. It was this process which enabled the patient and myself to explore the lack of differentiation between himself and his damaged parent. I found this phenomenon similar to the identification which takes place in pathological mourning. Freud (1917) described this identification as a process in which the person in mourning attempts to possess the object by becoming the object itself, rather than bearing a resemblance to it. This occurs when the person renounces the object while at the same time preserving it in a cannibalistic manner (Grinberg and Grinberg 1974; Green, 1986). This process, which the psychoanalytic literature describes as typical of Holocaust survivors' offspring is called 'primitive identification' (Freyberg, 1980; Grubrich-Simitis, 1984). It is this type of identification which is at the core of the offspring's inability to achieve self-differentiation and build a life of his own.

Some of the different types of traumatisations based on primitive identification which are relevant to the analytic material in this book are described below. While these modes of transmission may be universal, they bear the unique quality that the Holocaust experience imparted to them.

(a) *Traumatisation of the child by exploiting him as a vehicle for repeating the parent's trauma.* The parent creates a permeable membrane between himself and the child through which he transmits feelings of mourning and aggression which, because of their devastating nature, he cannot contain in himself or share with other adult partners. This process, which is actually a process of projective identification, serves to decrease the huge amount of self-destructiveness which could have been fatal to the parent (Gampel, 1986b; Kogan, 1989a).

(b) *Traumatisation through the emotional inaccessibility of the parent.* The child who attempts to comfort the parent by catering to his need for total empathy clings to an inaccessible parent

and thus forgoes the fulfilment of his own emotional needs.
The child initiates a kind of union with the needy parent in
order to nurture him, while actually seeking parenting for
himself (Auerhahn and Prelinger, 1983).

(c) *Traumatisation in fantasy.* This process occurs when the child,
in his endless efforts to understand his parent and thus help
him, tries to experience what the parent experienced by
recreating the traumatic experience and its accompanying
affects in fantasy (Auerhahn and Prelinger, 1983). Oliner
(1982), who explored hysterical character traits among
children of survivors, found a particular aspect of hysteria
described by Metcalf (1977) applicable to them; that is, 'the
parental expectations that the child be the protagonist in
scenes from the parents' unconscious fantasies – fantasies that
are almost always a sadistic distortion of narcissistic struggles
for survival with objects from the parents' past' (Metcalf, 1977,
p. 259). Traumatisation is the fulfilment of those parental
expectations.

(d) *Traumatisation through the loss of one's self.* Through a symbiotic
attachment to the child, the parent seeks the restitution of
his lost (often idealised) objects and the reparation of his
damaged self. The child, by sharing with his parent the
fantasy of denial of death and the miraculous restitution of
the lost objects, sacrifices his own individuality. If we compare
this again to the dynamics of hysteria, we find a similarity
between the loss of individuality of children of survivors
and the 'life of substitutions', described by Racamier (1952),
or the 'absence from oneself' referred to by Khan (1974).

Process II – The phenomenon of concretisation

The interplay between fantasy and reality in my patients' lives is
expressed through a phenomenon prominent among the offspring
of survivors which has been described by Bergmann (1982) and
labeled 'concretisation'. Concretisation refers to the fact that
these children, in their endless efforts to understand and help their
traumatised parents, try to experience what their parents have been
through by recreating their parents' experiences and accompanying affects in their own life. This phenomenon appears in all
of the case illustrations in this book.

Concretisation is especially apparent during the early stages of
analysis in patients whose parents underwent massive traumatisation and who set up psychological defences by denying their

own experiences. The children's unconscious fantasies around these experiences compelled them to live them out in their own life. This behavioural phenomenon results from the process of 'primitive identification' with the parents, described above.

I would like to briefly compare the phenomenon of concretisation with the phenomena of 'actualisation' (Sandler and Sandler, 1978) and the French school's *pensée operatoire* (Marty and de M'Uzan, 1983), both of which bear a certain similarity to concretisation.

Actualisation is a process through which an individual, rather than verbally asking another person to fulfil his wish, causes that person to act in a certain way in order to fulfil that wish.

Concretisation may be viewed as a sub-category of actualisation. It is a form of actualisation in which an individual causes another to act towards him in a certain way, by imposing upon the relationship fantasies linked to the parents' traumatic past. An example of this in the case illustrations presented in this book is Sara's exploitation of the love objects in her life, leading them to play the role of victim/aggressor, roles connected to her fantasies about her mother's past (Chapter VI).

Concretisation is similar to actualisation in its wish-fulfilling aspect. Concretisation refers to symbolic, displaced actions which are lived out with current real objects, but are unconsciously addressed to lost loved ones. It expresses an individual's striving towards realising an object-relationship with both real and fantasised objects. Concretisation differs from actualisation in that it applies only to traumatic themes from the past, which gives the need to concretise a particular urgency, whereas actualisation applies to a wider range of general themes, thus lacking the urgency of themes of death and survival.

An important function of concretisation is the avoidance of psychic pain. It is thus similar to the phenomenon of *pensée operatoire*. This phenomenon refers to a pragmatic way of thinking about people and events, and implies a lack of emotional response to crucial moments or traumatic losses in the lives of the people concerned. In this book, an example of this is Isaac (Chapter V), whose reactions to the catastrophic events in his life are devoid of emotion, his psychic condition bearing a resemblance to the phenomenon *pensée operatoire*. Isaac uses this mechanism to numb his feelings of depression and guilt and thus avoid mourning.

Concretisation bears a certain similarity to two other concepts described in the psychoanalytic literature dealing with Holocaust survivors' offspring: 'concretism' and 'transposition'.

Concretism is defined by Grubrich-Simitis (1984) as 'an impairment in the ego's capacity to use metaphor'. According to the author, living under the permanent threat of death brings primary needs of self-preservation to the fore, thus leaving no room for fantasy. This damage to the ego's capacity to form symbols and use metaphor can be transmitted by survivors to the second generation. Since survivors often blurred the real events, not establishing them in actual, non-metaphorical statements, their children were unable to learn to differentiate between the metaphorical and the non-metaphorical, between reality and fantasy. Another reason for the impediment or inadequate development of children's perception and differentiation of reality was the parents' unconscious repudiation of the children's fragmented perceptions through denial or disavowal.

Concretisation differs from concretism in that it is a behavioural phenomenon rather than an abstract concept. The children's impaired capacity to deal on a fantasy level with the traumatic experiences of their parents leads to their acting out in the present reality.

'Transposition' is a concept defined by Kestenberg (1982, 1989) as the second generation's fantasy of living during the Holocaust and rescuing the victims, but does not necessarily refer to the experiences of their parents.

Concretisation occurs in those patients who act out the traumatic aspects of their parents' lives without understanding what they are doing. Concretisation is broader in scope than transposition, since it symbolises bringing someone back to life or causing their death. It therefore includes not only the offspring's attempt to rescue the victims, but also the wish to destroy them, as a result of identifying with the aggressor.

The themes of 'transposition' or 'concretisation' illustrate the pervasive and persistent presence of the Holocaust which dominates the inner landscapes of survivors' children. Both themes appear in the description of psychotherapeutic work with children of survivors of many authors (Wardi, 1992; Laub and Auerhahn, 1993; Wilson, 1985; Auerhahn and Prelinger, 1983; Gampel, 1982; Herzog, 1982; Freyberg, 1980; Kestenberg, 1980).

It is in the process of psychoanalysis that these children come to understand the many meanings of the parents' past, and its profound influence on their own psychological development. Grubrich-Simitis (1984) describes the task of the analyst in therapy with children of survivors as helping the patient to learn that 'what takes place in this world is serious, but not deadly serious; speaking and fantasising are not equated with doing'.

Cahn (1987) hypothesised that Holocaust survivors' inability to acknowledge or verbalise their experience affects their children's symbolising capacities, making it more difficult for children to 'translate their own experiences of their parents and of their feelings into words'.

Adelman (1993) proposed that 'overwhelming or disorganising affective states profoundly influence the capacity to verbalise and acknowledge experience ...'

Through my clinical experience, I found that the 'second generation' patients were able to translate their concretisations into a cognitive mode only during the more advanced stages of treatment. During these phases I was able, by means of my interpretations, to help the patient achieve insight into these re-enactments. Through them, the patient begins to understand the unconscious meaning of his actions and verbalise it. In the various analyses in this book, and especially in Chapter VII, insight is a tool for helping these patients extricate themselves from concretisation.

The Construction of a New, Separate and More Cohesive Self by Means of the Therapeutic Relationship

The second central theme in the analyses of second generation survivors described in this book is their struggle for a life of their own, and the resulting birth of a new, separate and more cohesive self. Below is a general description of the phases of this process[11] as they occur within the therapeutic relationship. Throughout the different phases I put forward my own particular way of being present with the patient, listening and interpreting as a means for achieving this aim.

Phase I

The patient often comes for treatment after experiencing a second traumatisation which may represent a resurgence, a continuation of the transmitted trauma. At the same time this presents the patient with a new opportunity in which the predetermined direction of the flow of his internal psychic life can be shifted and reorganised.

Treatment after a second traumatisation often begins with a phase of incomprehensibility. We see fragments upon fragments re-enacted; concretisations that make no sense. Isaac (Chapter V), in his attempt to injure himself, in injuring his father, and in his subsequent psychotic state, is the example *par excellence* of this phase.

In the midst of this chaos of meaning, a signal is given, a password, a hint, which must be picked up. Such a password can be found in disorganised drawings (Kay, Chapter III) or in dreams (Sara's dream of drinking milk with ashes, Chapter VI). The password indicates the existence of an engulfing 'hole', a threat, or, to use Grossman's (1986) symbolic name for the Holocaust, a 'Beast' – something which the patient cannot deal with.

The patient experiences this 'hole', which represents a part of his parent's history which has disappeared, as a persistent wound in his psyche or a gap in his emotional understanding. This 'psychic hole' does not belong to the category of 'blankness' – negative hallucination, blank psychosis, blank mourning, all connected to what Green (1986) calls the problem of emptiness or of the negative. The 'psychic hole' I am talking about is more similar to the 'black hole' in the world of physics, a body which sucks into itself everything that gets close to it because of the forces of gravitation. The 'psychic hole' is also a body, the encapsulation of the fantasy of the traumatic past of parents, which has an impact on the whole life of the patient.

The uniqueness of the 'psychic hole' in cases of second-generation patients is in the way it is formed and the way it leaves traces in the unconscious. In contrast to the 'psychic hole' created in the self by the denial or repression of one's own traumatic experiences, the 'psychic hole', in cases of Holocaust survivors' offspring, is formed through the denial or repression of the trauma by their parents (a trauma which, by means of 'primitive identification', becomes attributed to themselves), as well as through the offspring's repression of the traces of the trauma. I believe that in cases in which the parents have succeeded in working through feelings of mourning and guilt connected to their traumatic past, and in conveying their history to the children in a healthier way, the children tend much less to experience a 'psychic hole' in their psychic reality.

Let us try to understand this phenomenon. Even in those families in which the 'pact of silence' prevails, the child will still be able to guess some of the details of the parents' severe traumatisation. When cognitive development is sufficiently advanced, he or she will start to investigate the parents' past. At this stage the parents' wish to deny or repress the traumatic events could force them unconsciously to convey to the searching child that the object of their investigation is not something that really happened in their lives. Rather it is the child's wicked thought, a bad dream, something that ought to be forgotten (Grubrich-Simitis, 1984). Thus, the parents' redefinition of the traumatic events in their lives as something horrible coming from the child's inner world makes the reality of the trauma unreal.

Through these processes, what was known or almost known becomes 'unknown'. It is the 'unknown', or that which cannot be remembered, which is the source of the child's unconscious fantasies about his parent's traumatic past, and his compelling need to act them out in his present life.

Suffering from a 'hole' in his psychic structure, the patient often lives on the brink of an 'unthinkable anxiety' (Winnicott, 1962). This anxiety takes on various forms in the different case illustrations in this book: (a) going to pieces (Kay's fear of 'falling apart', Chapter III); (b) falling for ever (Sara's fear of marriage as falling into a 'limitless black hole', Chapter VI); (c) not relating to the body (Josepha's numbing of her physical pain, Chapter IV); and (d) disorientation (Isaac's psychic condition after shooting and wounding his father, Chapter V).

In such cases it is the analyst's task to first alleviate the patient's anxiety, then to support him in confronting the 'hole' and finally help him 'repair' it. To quote Kinston and Cohen (1986): 'Hole repair is what psychoanalytic therapy is about.'

In order to decrease the patient's anxiety and give him a sense of security about his existence, the analyst has to create a 'holding relationship'[12], a nurturing, confiding and reflecting relationship which is characterised by an intense emotional attachment and deep empathic communication.

Communication in the first phase of treatment is often on a non-verbal level and is based on over-sensitive rapport: the analyst has to know how the patient feels and what he is thinking without the patient communicating these feeling and thoughts in words.

This over-sensitive rapport, this intimate, valid and nourishing type of relationship is the only kind of relationship that has any meaning for the patient and it cements the therapeutic work alliance.

Like the mother who instinctively knows what her baby needs, it is vitally important at this stage that the analyst place himself in the patient's shoes so that he can intuitively know what he needs. The analyst must often change his normal procedure in order to meet the patient's needs without immediately inter-preting his underlying, unconscious wishes. An example of this is when I had to adapt the analytic setting to the needs of the patient (for example, when I agreed to see Josepha sporadically, on 'her terms', until she was able to come back regularly to analysis, Chapter IV; Kay communicating with me through drawings, Chapter III). The delay in my attempt to interpret what is happening is parallel to the situation described by Winnicott (1965) in his model of infant and child care, of the mother holding the child who has an ear-ache in her arms, since soothing words are of no use.

I believe that the more concrete form of holding is especially necessary in the first stage of treatment of second-generation patients, since they often place their lives in real or imagined danger. It is only through the empathic communication which takes place mainly on a non-verbal level that the analyst can convey his caring and involvement to the patient and thus provide him with some security in analysis as well as in life, leading to the strengthening of his psychic forces.

Phase II

Now that the patient has become stronger, his struggle to face the 'Beast' can begin to surface. Analysis undergoes a series of crises, a test to see whether the analyst is indeed 'present' and strong enough to face the 'Beast', a test of whether life can vanquish death. This test consists of the patient's attempt to destroy the analyst's prowess and castrate him in his analytic role. At this point, the analytic relationship is often in danger of being broken.

Through the various case illustrations, we can observe my recurring reaction during this difficult phase. First I attempt to explore my countertransference feelings and find that my nar-cissistic hurt is mainly due to the patient's rejection, especially since we have both already made an emotional investment in the treatment which has been going on for a considerable amount of time. Following this, I often feel helpless when confronted with the patient's destructive attack. By working through my feelings, I realise time and time again that my feelings of impotence and lack of hope through this period are the patient's own feelings in confronting the 'Beast', which are powerfully projected upon me and with which I am identifying. My gradual awareness of this fact helps me arrive at the conclusion that surviving the patient's attack (that is, my continuing to function as an analyst without retaliating) is vital for the patient's well-being (Winnicott, 1971). This helps me remain 'alive and whole', and resume the therapeutic role. The therapeutic relationship is mended and strengthened, and the treatment continues after a shorter or longer break.

I find this break in the therapeutic relationship a phenomenon worth exploring, since it is characteristic of many second-generation patients. It is possible that the break creates a hole in the treatment which symbolises the hole in the patient's psyche. Through his acting out, the patient unconsciously conveys to the therapist his own feelings of lack of self-coherence. The patient's experience of a 'wound' in his psyche is expressed in this phase in a concrete form by wounding the therapeutic relationship. The analyst's survival of this test goes a long way in allowing for the next, more open phase to emerge. It is the analyst's own survival which, for the patient, is an actual victory over death.

The analytic work up until now paves the way for the third phase in which empathy and understanding can be conveyed in a more mature form, through words.

Phase III

The special aspect of this phase is my particular way of interpreting the patient's unconscious thoughts and feelings. I believe that my interpretations are mutative in the sense that they lead the patient to mobilise life-forces against the 'Beast' and, in turn, to an affirmation of his own life.

Thus, in analysis, when we both, patient and analyst alike, encounter the 'Thanatic object', the 'Beast' – the mental representation of the atrocities of the Holocaust which is often linked to an actual trauma in the patient's own life – I participate with the patient in his struggle against it. My interpretations convey not only the fact that I understand the deepest anxieties experienced by the patient in his confrontation with the 'Beast', but also, like the mother who holds her distressed baby in her arms, they convey a soothing, life-giving embrace. To quote Freud in a letter to Jung: 'Psychoanalysis is in essence a cure through love.' It is Eros, the life-force, which is conveyed through the analyst's words which often stems the tide of Thanatos, the death-force. My knowledge and understanding of the power of Thanatos has greatly enabled me, by use of mutative interpretations, to help my patients achieve a deeper appreciation of life. That is not to say that Thanatos is disappearing from their lives, but that it becomes tamed by the life-force and comes under its control.

As can be seen in the various case illustrations, these mutative interpretations usually arrest the flow of fragmentary re-enactments and crises, and there is a moment of silence, of self-reflection and discovery, often filled with a sense of absence and void. The cry that has been hidden, the affect of the Holocaust has broken through!

From the mute cry at the start, and along the continuation of the analytic process, through the ongoing intimate dialogue, a comprehensible narrative evolves. What emerges is a story of real events (for example, Isaac's father's story about the execution of his own father which he and his mother were witness to, Chapter V; Josepha's mother's story of distress when she believed her mother was killed by the Nazis, Chapter IV). It is a narrative that emerges hauntingly in a newly-found analytic relationship.

In some cases, the story doesn't emerge easily, but has to be actively sought. The analyst's supportive attitude helps the patient search for the 'unknown' belonging to his parent's past. The integration of the 'unknown' can only occur now, when the ego is strong enough to tolerate the pain of the repressed affects associated with the parent's history. The patient becomes able to find that part of history that will fill the 'hole' by searching for concrete details from his parent's past (Kay asking for her father's book of memoirs, Chapter III; Sara breaking her mother's locked cupboard in order to steal her diary, Chapter VI).

This quest for information, whose purpose is that the patient give up living with the shadows of the past, is a difficult experience for the survivor's child and is accompanied by great anxiety. Consciously, the child is afraid that his questions about the past will force the parent to re-experience painful, traumatic memories, which may threaten his psychic survival. Unconsciously, the child experiences his wish to know his parent's history as a step towards differentiation and relief from the burden of the past, a fact which he feels might be potentially destructive to the parent.

This search is usually facilitated by the holding atmosphere in analysis, and by the patient taking the analyst on as an ally in this quest.

Both analyst and patient eagerly await the story which emerges from this quest, and after its rendition and its working-through, living in a real world becomes possible for the patient. The terrifying 'hole' has been filled by a more comprehensible, although very painful, story, thus completing the circle. Treatment does not always end here, but a better integrated, separate self has been born.

Thus the work presented in this book is a progression from the interpretation of fragmentary, defensive re-enactments to an awareness of the reality of trauma, that allows it to become part of the flow of life, and thus allows life to be more whole.

Notes

1. Excerpts of this case study were presented at the 34th IPA Congress, Hamburg, 1985, under the title 'Identification and denial in the shadow of Nazism'. Published in *Psychoanalyse in Exil – Texte Verfolgter Analytiker*, eds S. Broser and G. Pagel. Wurzburg: Konigshausen and Neumann, pp. 128–39, 1987. Published in the *International Journal of Psychoanalysis* (1986) 67: 45–52. Also in *Sigmund Freud House Bulletin* (1989) 13(2): 25–35 and in *Psyche – Zeitschrift fur Psychoanalyse und ihre Anwendungen* (1990) 44 Jahrgang IV: 533–44, in an expanded paper entitled 'Working through the vicissitudes of trauma in the psychoanalyses of Holocaust survivors' offspring'.
2. The concept 'Mythos of Survival' (Klein, 1981) describes a longitudinal process in which a person, traumatised by Holocaust experiences, creates personal myths or fantasies which are different from other types of neuroses. These myths contain memories from the past and have the function of preserving a traumatic screen in the sense used by Kris (1956), i.e. sometimes hiding massive amounts of ambivalence and hostility which can be unleashed by brutality, anxiety or emotional pathology. This process, which began during the Holocaust, continues to influence the survivor at different stages in his life cycle. It has an influence on his perception of his body image, his object relations, his political views and the way he relates to problems of life and death. The 'Mythos of Survival' is the realisation of conflictual emotions and unconscious wishes regarding living or dying.
3. An abbreviated form of this chapter was presented at the 35th IPA Congress, Montreal, 1987, under the title 'Analysis terminable and interminable – Eros and Thanatos at strife'. Published in the *International Journal of Psychoanalysis* (1989) 70: 661–71, under the name 'The search for self'. Also in

Sigmund Freud House Bulletin (1989) 13(2): 25–35; and in *Psyche – Zeitschrift fur Psychoanalyse und ihre Anwendungen* (1990) 44 Jahrgang IV: 533–44, in an enlarged paper entitled 'Working through the vicissitudes of trauma in the psycho-analyses of Holocaust survivors' offspring'.

4. This chapter was presented in an abbreviated form at the 35th IPA Congress, Montreal, 1987, and at a meeting of the Freudian Contemporary Group, London, 1987. Published in the *International Review of Psychoanalysis*, 1987, 15: 251–9, and in *Libro Anual de Psicoanalisis* (1988). The title of this chapter is based on Bick's paper 'The experience of the skin in early object-relations' (1968), although there it has a different connotation.

5. This chapter was presented at the International Conference of Psychological and Psychiatric Sequelae of Nazi Terror in Aging Survivors and their Offspring, Hanover, 1989; at the 5th Annual Meeting of the Society for Traumatic Stress Studies on Learning from Victims/Survivors: Insight, Intervention and Care, San Francisco, 1990. It was published in the *International Journal of Psychoanalysis* (1980) 71: 629–40; in *Libro Anual de Psicoanalisis* (1990); and also in *Zeitschrift fur Psychoanalytische Theorie und Praxis* (1991), Jahrgang VI(1): 62–79.

6. We can conceive of this behaviour also as 'acting in', a term which refers to acting out within the treatment situation (Zeligs, 1957; Rosen, 1965; Eidelberg, 1968).

7. Paper presented at the 4th International Conference on Psychological Stress and Adjustment in Time of War and Peace, Tel Aviv, 1989; at the 2nd International Conference of Wartime Medical Services, Stockholm, 1990; at the EPF Conference, Stockholm, 1991; at the Michael Balint Institut, Hamburg, 1991. Published in the *International Journal of Psychoanalysis* (1992), 73: 455–65. Also in *Psychoanalysis in Europe* (1992), 39: 3–21.

8. An abbreviated form of this chapter was presented at the EPF Conference, Vienna, 1993, under the title 'Listening to the Sound of Mute Children'; also at the Sigmund Freud Institut, Frankfurt, 1993; at the International Congress on Persecution, War and Children, Hamburg, 1993. The full version was presented at the IPA Congress, Amsterdam, 1993. Published in the *International Journal of Psychoanalysis* (forthcoming) 1995 under the title 'Love and the heritage of the past".

9. This chapter is based on a paper presented at the Bi-Annual Conference of the D.P.V., Wiesbaden, November 1991; Also presented at the S.P.P., Paris, July, 1992. Published in the *International Journal of Psychoanalysis* (1993), 74: 803–04; all of the above under the title 'Curative factors in the psychoanalyses of Holocaust survivors' offspring before and during the Gulf War'.
10. It should be pointed out no one has ever been able to find this definition in a written statement of Freud's, but Erikson cites Freud as having said something to this effect in *Childhood and Society* (1951, p.229).
11. This section is based in part on Dr. D. Laub's discussion of my work 'Love and the heritage of the past', which he presented at the IPA Congress, Amsterdam, 1993.
12. The analyst's function of 'holding' (Winnicott, 1965) appears in the psychoanalytic literature under different formulations: Balint's 'primary object'; Hartmann's 'average expectable environment'; Bion's 'container'; Little's 'basic unit'; Khan's 'protective shield'; Spitz's 'mediator of environment'; Mahler's 'extra-uterine matrix'. I have chosen Winnicott's term 'holding' for describing the way the analyst attempts to help the growth of the patient's self, because it is closest to the mother's way of facilitating the development of the infant's self at the beginning of life.

Bibliography

Adelman, A. (1993) 'Representation and remembrance: on retelling inherited narratives of the Holocaust'. Unpublished doctoral dissertation, City University, New York.

Anthony, E.J. and Koupernik, C. (eds) (1973) *The Child in His Family: The Impact of Disease and Death*. New York: John Wiley.

Anzieu, D. (1985) *Le Moi-Peau*. Paris: Dunod.

Auerhahn, N.C. and Prelinger, E. (1983) 'Repetition in the concentration camp survivor and her child', *Int. Rev. Psycho-Anal.* 10: 31–45.

Axelrod, S.; Schnipper, O.L. and Rau, J.H. (1978) 'Hospitalised offspring of Holocaust survivors: problems and dynamics'. Paper presented at the Annual Meeting of the American Psychiatric Association, Atlanta, May 1978.

Axline, V.M. (1969) *Play Therapy*. New York: Balantine.

Bak, R.C. (1973) 'Being in love and object loss', *International Journal of Psychoanalysis*. 54: 1–8.

Balint, M. (1948) 'On genital love', in *Primary Love and Psychoanalytic Technique*. London: Tavistock, 1953, pp. 109–20.

—— (1952) 'New beginning and the paranoid and depressive syndromes', in *Primary Love and Psychoanalytic Technique*. London: Hogarth, 1952.

Barocas, H.A. and Barocas, C.B. (1973) 'Manifestations of concentration camp effects on the second generation'. *American Journal of Psychiatry* 130: 820–1.

Bergmann, M.S. (1971) 'Psychoanalytic observations on the capacity to love', in J.B. McDewitt and C.F. Settlage, eds. *Separation – Individuation*. New York: International University Press, pp. 15–40.

—— and Jucovy, M.E. (eds) (1982) *Generations of the Holocaust*. New York: Basic.

165

Bergmann, M.V. (1982) 'Thoughts on super-ego pathology of survivors and their children', in M.S. Bergmann and M.E. Jucovy, eds. *Generations of the Holocaust*. New York: Basic, pp. 287–311.

Bick, E. (1968) 'The experience of the skin in early object-relations', *International Journal of Psychoanalysis* 49: 484–6.

Bion, R. (1955) 'Language and the schizophrenic', in M. Klein, P. Heimann and R. Money-Kyhle, eds, *New Directions in Psychoanalysis*. London: Tavistock, pp. 220–40.

Brody, S. (1973) 'The son of a refugee', *Psychoanal. Study Child* 28: 169–91.

Cahn, A. (1987) 'The capacity to acknowledge experience in Holocaust survivors and their children', Unpublished doctoral dissertation, Adelphi University.

Chasseguet-Smirgel, J. (1986) 'The archaic matrix of the Oedipus Complex', in *Sexuality and Mind*. New York and London: University Press.

—— (1989) 'Some reflections of a psychoanalyst on the Nazi biocracy and genocide', *Int. Rev. Psycho-Anal.* 17: 167–72.

Eidelberg, L. (ed.) (1968) *Encyclopedia of Psychoanalysis*. New York: Free Press.

Erikson, E.H. (1951) *Childhood and Society*. Harmondsworth: Penguin (1965).

Erikson, E.H. (1956) 'The problem of ego identity', *J. Amer. Psychoanal. Assn* 4: 56–121.

—— (1950) *Childhood and Society*. New York: Norton.

Felman, S. and Laub, O. (1992) *Testimony. Crises of Witnessing in Literature, Psychoanalysis and History*. New York and London: Routledge.

Ferenczi, S. (1920) 'The further development of an active therapy in psychoanalysis', in *Further Contributions to the Theory and Technique of Psychoanalysis*. London: Hogarth, 1926.

Ficowski, J. (1981) *A Reading of Ashes*, trans. Keith Bosley and Krystyna Wandycz. London:Mermaid P.R. p. 2.

Fogelman, E. (1988) 'Intergenerational group therapy: Child survivors of the Holocaust and offspring of survivors', *Psychoanal. Rev.* 75(4): 619–40.

Fresco, N. (1984) 'Remembering the unknown', *Int. Rev. Psycho-Anal.* 11: 417–27.

Freud, S. (1895) 'Project for a scientific psychology', in James Strachey, ed. *The Standard Edition of the Complete Psychological*

Works of Sigmund Freud, 24 vols. London: Hogarth, 1953–73, vol. 1.

—— (1912) 'On the universal tendency to debasement in the sphere of love', *S.E.*11.

—— (1915a) ;The unconscious', *S.E.*14.

—— (1915b) 'Repression', *S.E.*14.

—— (1915c) 'Thoughts for the time of war and death', (1) The disillusionment of the war. *S.E.*14.

—— (1917) 'Mourning and melancholi', *S.E.*14.

—— (1919) 'A child is being beaten: a contribution to the study of the origin of sexual perversions', *S.E.*17.

—— (1920) 'Beyond the pleasure principle', *S.E.*8.

—— (1923) 'The ego and the id', *S.E.*19.

—— (1924) 'The loss of reality in neurosis and psychosis', *S.E.*19.

—— (1926) 'Inhibitions, symptoms and anxiety', *S.E.*20.

Freyberg, J. (1989) 'The emerging self in the survivor family', in *Healing their Wounds: Psychotherapy with Holocaust Survivors and their Families*. New York: Praeger.

Freyberg, S. (1980) 'Difficulties in separation – individuation, as experienced by offspring of Nazi Holocaust survivors', *American Journal of Orthopsychiatry* 5: 87–95.

Fromm, E. (1962) *The Art of Loving*. London: Unwin, p. 47.

Furman, E. (1973) 'The impact of the Nazi concentration camps on the children of survivors', in E.J. Anthony and C. Koupernik, eds. *The Child in His Family: The Impact of Disease and Death*. New York: John Wiley, 2: 379–84.

Gampel, Y. (1982) 'A daughter of silence', in M.S. Bergmann and M.E. Jucovy eds. *Generations of the Holocaust*, New York: Basic, pp. 120–36.

—— (1986a) 'La vie, la mort et le prenom d'un enfant', in P. Fedida and J. Guyota eds *Actualites Transgenerationelles en Psychopathologie*, Paris: Echo-Centurion, pp. 123–31.

—— (1986b) 'L'effrayent et le menacant: de la transmission a la repetition', Paris: *Psychoanalyse à L'Université*, No 2, 11, 41: 87–102.

Gebirtig, M. (1937) *Meine Lieder*.

Glover, E. (1937) 'Symposium on the theory and the therapeutic results of psychoanalysis', *International Journal of Psychoanalysis* 18: 125–89.

—— (1956a) 'Development of the body ego', *Psychoanal. Study Child* 5: 19–23.

—— (1956b) *On the Early Development of the Mind*. New York: International University Press.

——; Fenichel, O.; Strachey, J.; Bergler, E.; Nunberg, H. and Bibring, E. (1937) 'Symposium on the theory and the therapeutic results of Psychoanalysis', *International Journal of Psychoanalysis* 18: 125–89.

Green, A. (1986) 'The dead mother', in *On Private Madness*. London: Hogarth.

Greenacre, P. (1967) 'The influence of infantile trauma on genetic patterns', in S.S. Furst, ed. *Psychic Trauma*, New York and London: Basic.

Grinberg, L. (1964) 'Two kinds of guilt – their relations with normal and pathological aspects of mourning', *International Journal of Psychoanalysis* 45: 366–71.

—— (1968) 'On acting out and its role in the psychoanalytic process', *International Journal of Psychoanalysis* 49: 171–8.

—— (1992) *Guilt and Depression*. London and New York: Karnac.

—— and Grinberg, R. (1974) 'The problem of identity and the psychoanalytical process', *International Journal of Psychoanalysis* 1: 499–507.

Grubrich-Simitis, I. (1984) 'From concretism to metaphor', *Psychoanal. Study Child* 39: 301–19.

Grossman, D. (1986) *See Under Love*. Tel-Aviv: Hakibbutz Hameuchad.

Guntrip, P.M. (1980) *Schizoid Phenomena, Object Relations and the Self*. London: Hogarth.

Herzog, J. (1982) 'World beyond metaphor: Thoughts on the transmission of trauma', in M. Bergmann and M. Jucovy, eds. *Generations of the Holocaust*, New York: Basic.

Hoffer, W. (1950) 'Development of the body ego', *Psychoanal. Study Child* 5: 19–23.

Hoppe, K. (1962) 'Persecution, depression and aggression', *Bulletin Menninger Clinic* 26: 195–203.

Houzel, D. (1987) 'The concept of psychic envelope', in Didier Anzieu, ed. *Psychic Envelopes*, London: Karnac, 1990.

Jacobson, E. (1964) *The Self and the Object World*. New York: International University Press.

Joffe, W.G. and Sandler, J. (1965) 'Pain, depression and individuation', in J. Sandler, ed. *From Safety to Superego*, London: Karnac, 1987.

Joseph, B. (1989) in Michael Feldman and Elisabeth Bott Spillius, eds. *Psychic Equilibrium and Psychic Change*. New Library of Psychoanalysis. London and New York: Tavistock/Routledge.

Josselyn, I.M. (1971) 'The capacity to love – a possible reformulation', *Journal of American Academy Child Psychiatry* 10: 6–22.

Jucovy, M.E. (1992) 'Psychoanalytic contributions to Holocaust studies', *International Journal of Psychoanalysis* 73: 267–83.

Kernberg, O. (1974) 'Barrier to falling and remaining in love', *J. Amer. Psychoanal. Assn* 4: 743–68.

—— (1976) 'Mature love: prerequisites and characteristics', in *Object Relations Theory and Clinical Psychoanalysis*. New Jersey and London: Jason Aronson, pp. 215–41.

—— (1986) 'Identification in psychosis', *International Journal of Psychoanalysis* 67: 147–59.

Kestenberg, J.S. (1972a) 'How children remember and parents forget', *International Journal of Psychoanalytic Psychotherapy* 1–2: 103–23.

—— (1972b) 'Psychoanalytic contributions to the problem of children of survivors from Nazi persecution', *Israeli Annals of Psychiatry* 10: 311–25.

—— (1980) 'Psychoanalyses of children of survivors from the Holocaust: case presentations and assessment', *J. Amer. Psychoanal. Assn* 28: 775–804.

—— (1982) 'A metapyschological assessment based on an analysis of a survivor's child', in M.S. Bergmann and M.E. Jucovy, eds. *Generations of the Holocaust*, New York: Basic, pp. 137–58.

—— (1989) 'Transposition revisited: clinical, therapeutic and developmental considerations', in P. Marcus and A. Rosenberg, eds. *Healing their Wounds: Psychotherapy with Holocaust Survivors and their Families*, New York: Praeger, pp. 67–82.

Khan, M. and Masud, R. (1974) 'La rancune de l'hysterique', *Nouvelle Revue de Psychoanalyse* 10: 151–8.

Kinston, W. and Cohen, J. (1986) 'Primal repression: clinical and theoretic aspects', *International Journal of Psychoanalysis* 67: 337–57.

Klein, H. (1971) 'Families of Holocaust survivors in the kibbutz: psychological studies', in H. Krystal and W.G. Niederland, eds. *Psychic Traumatisation: After-effects in Individuals and Communities*, Boston: Little and Brown.

—— (1973a) 'Children of the Holocaust: mourning and bereavement', in E.J. Anthony and C. Koupernick, eds. *The Child in His*

Family: The Impact of Disease and Death. New York: John Wiley, pp. 393–409.

—— (1973b) 'Delayed effects and after-effects of severe traumatisation', *Israel Journal of Psychiatry and Related Sciences* 10: 188–225.

—— (1981) Yale Symposium on the Holocaust. Proceedings, September, 1981.

—— and Kogan, I. (1986) 'Identification and denial in the shadow of Nazis', *International Journal of Psychoanalysis* 67: 45–52. Reprinted in Stephen Brose and Gerda Pagel, eds. *Pyschoanalyse im Exil – Texte Verfolgter Analytiker.* Wurzburg: Konigshausen and Neumann (1987), pp. 128–37.

Klein, M. (1932) *The Psychoanalysis of Children.* In the *Writings of Melanie Klein*, vol. 2, London: Hogarth (1975).

—— (1940) 'Mourning and its relation to manic depressive states', In *The Writings of J. Melanie Klein* I, London: Hogarth (1975).

Kogan, I. (1987) 'The second skin', *Int. Rev. Psycho-Anal.* 15: 251–61. Reprinted in *Libro Anual de Psicoanalisis* 1988; in Jutta Gutwinsky-Jeggle and Johann Michael Rotmann, eds. *Die kluge Sinne pflegend – Psychoanalytische und kulturkritische Beitrage. Hermann Beland zu Ehren.* Tubingen: Edition Diskord (1993), pp. 309–26.

—— (1989a) 'Working through the vicissitudes of trauma in the psychoanalyses of Holocaust survivors' offspring', *Psychotherapeutisch Passpoort* 3: (1), 53–68; *The Sigmund Freud House Bulletin*, vol. 13(2), winter, 1989; *Psyche, Zeitschrift fur Psychoanalyse und ihre Anwendungen* 1990, 6: 533–45.

—— (1989b) 'The search for self', *International Journal of Psychoanalysis* 70: 661–71.

—— (1990) 'A journey to pain', *International Journal of Psychoanalysis* 1: 629–40. Reprinted in *Libro Anual de Psicoanalisis* 1991; in *Zeitschrift fur Psychoanalytische Theorie und Praxis*, Jahrgang VI(1), 1991.

—— (1991) 'From acting out to words and meaning', *International Journal of Psychoanalysis* 73: 455–67; *Psychoanalysis in Europe*, Bulletin 39, autumn 1992, pp. 3–21.

—— (1993) 'Curative factors in the psychoanalyses of Holocaust survivors' offspring before and during the Gulf War', *International Journal of Psychoanalysis* 74: 803–15; in Gertrud Hardtmann, ed. *Spuren der Verfolgung*, Gerlingen: Bleicher, 1992.

—— (1995) 'Love and the heritage of the past', paper presented at the IPA Congress, Amsterdam, 1993, *International Journal of Psychoanalysis* (1995) (forthcoming).

Krell, R. (1979) 'Holocaust families: The survivors and their children', *Comprehensive Psychiatry* 20(6): 560–7.

Kris, E. (1956) 'The personal myth: a problem in psychoanalytic technique', *J. Amer. Psychoanal. Assn* 4: 653–81; in *Selected Papers of Ernst Kris*. New Haven: Yale University Press, 1975, pp. 201–340.

Laplanche, J. and Pontalis, J.P. (1967) *The Language of Psychoanalysis*. New York: Norton, 1973.

Laub, D. (1993) Discussion of Kogan's paper 'Love and the heritage of the past'. Presented at the IPA Congress, Amsterdam, 1993.

—— and Auerhahn, N.C. (1984) 'Reverberations of genocide: its expression in the conscious and unconscious of post-Holocaust generations', in Steven A. Luel and Paul Marcus, eds. *Psychoanalytic Reflections on the Holocaust: Selected Essays*, New York: University of Denver and Ktav.

—— (1993) 'Knowing and not knowing massive psychic trauma: forms of traumatic memory', *International Journal of Psychoanalysis* 74: 287–302.

Laufer, M. (1973) 'The analysis of a child of survivors', in E.J. Anthony and C. Koupernik, eds. *The Child in His Family: The Impact of Disease and Death*, New York: John Wiley, 2: 363–73.

Levine, H. (1982) 'Toward a psychoanalytic understanding of children of survivors of the Holocaust', *Psychoanal. Q.* 51: 70–92.

Levine, H.B. (1985) 'Psychotherapy as the initial phase of psychoanalysis', *Int. Rev. Psycho-Anal.* 12: 285–97.

Lifton, R. (1978) 'Witnessing survival', *Transactions* March–April, pp. 40–4.

Lipkowitz, M.H. (1973) 'The child of two survivors: the report of an unsuccessful therapy', *Israeli Annals of Psychiatry and Related Disciplines*, 11: 2.

Loftus, E.F. and Loftus, G.R. (1980) 'On the permanence of stored information on the human brain', *American Psychologist*, 5: 405–20.

Mahler, M.S. (1968) *On Human Symbiosis and the Vicissitudes of Individuation*. vol. 1, 'Infantile Psychosis'. New York: International University Press.

—— (1975) *The Psychological Birth of the Human Infant*. New York: Basic.

Marty, P. and De M'uzan, M. (1983) 'La pensee operatoire', *Revue Français de Psychanalyse* 27: 345–56.

May, R. (1969) *Love and Will*. New York: Norton.

Melzer, D. (1967) *The Psychoanalytical Process*. Perthshire, Scotland: Clunie.

Metcalf, A. (1977) 'Childhood: from process to structure', in Horowitz, ed. *Hysterical Personality*, pp. 223–81.

Michaux, H. (1944) *L'Espace du Dedans*. Pous: Gallimard, 3rd ed.

Milner, M. (1952) 'Aspects of symbolism in the comprehension of the not-self', *International Journal of Psychoanalysis* 33: 181–95.

—— (1993a) in R. Moses, ed. *Persistent Shadows of the Holocaust – The Meaning to Those Not Directly Affected*. New York: International University Press.

Moses, R. (1978) 'Adult psychic trauma: the question of early predisposition and some detailed mechanism', *International Journal of Psychoanalysis* 59: 353–63.

—— (1993a) *Persistent Shadows of the Holocaust – The Meaning to Those Not Directly Affected*. New York: International University Press.

—— (1993b) Discussion of M. Sebek's paper 'Aggression on the couch and aggression in the state', presented at the Annual Conference of the Israel Psychotherapy Association, Tel Aviv, 1993.

Nacht, S. (1962) 'The curative factors in psychoanalysis', *International Journal of Psychoanalysis* 43: 206–11.

Niederland, W. (1968) 'The problem of the survivor', in H. Kyrstal, ed. *Massive Psychic Trauma*. New York: International University Press.

Oliner, M.M. (1982) 'Hysterical features among children of survivors', in M.S. Bergmann and M.E. Jucovy, eds. *Generations of the Holocaust*, New York: Basic, pp. 267–85.

Peskin, H., Auerhahn, N.C. and Laub, D. (1995) 'The second Holocaust: therapeutic rescue', *Psyche, Zeitschrift fur Psychoanalyse und ihre Anwendungen* (forthcoming).

Phillips, R. (1978) 'Impact of the Nazi Holocaust on children of survivors', *American Journal of Psychotherapy* 32: 370–7.

Pines, D. (1980) 'Skin communication: early skin disorders and their effect on transference and countertransference', *International Journal of Psychoanalysis* 61: 315–22; in *A Woman's Unconscious Use of her Body – A Psychoanalytical Perspective*. London: Virago, 1993.

—— (1986) 'Working with women survivors of the Holocaust', *International Journal of Psychoanalysis* 67: 295–306; in *A Woman's Unconscious Use of her Body – A Psychoanalytical Perspective.* London: Virago, 1993.

—— (1993) 'The impact of the Holocaust on the second generation', in *A Woman's Unconscious Use of her Body – A Psychoanalytical Perspective.* London: Virago.

Pontalis, J.B. (1981) *Frontiers in Psychoanalysis: Between the Dream and Psychic Pain.* New York: International University Press.

Racamier, P.C. (1952) 'Hysterie et theatre', in *De Psychoanalyse en Psychiatrie.* Paris: Payot, pp. 135–64.

Rakoff, V. (1966) 'Long-term effects of the concentration camp experience', *Viewpoints* 1: 17–21.

—— (1969) 'Children and families of concentration camp survivors', *Canada's Mental Health* 14: 24–6.

Riviere, J. (1955) 'The unconscious fantasy of an inner world reflected in examples from literature', in M. Klein, P. Heimann and R. Money-Kyhle, eds *New Directions in Psychoanalysis.* London: Tavistock, pp. 346–70.

Rosen, J. (1965) 'The concept of "acting out"', in L. Abt and S. Weissman, eds. *Acting Out*, New York: Grune and Stratton.

Rosenfeld, D. (1986) 'Identification and its vicissitudes in relation to the Nazi phenomenon', *International Journal of Psychoanalysis* 67: 53–64.

Sandler, A.M. (1977) 'Beyond eight month anxiety', *International Journal of Psychoanalysis* 58: 195–207.

—— (1985) 'The structure of transference interpretation in clinical practice'. Paper presented to a Conference on Varieties of Transference Interpretation, Sigmund Freud Centre, Hebrew University, Jerusalem, 1985.

Sandler, J. and Sandler, A.M. (1978) 'On the development of object-relations and affects', *International Journal of Psychoanalysis* 59: 285–93.

Schaeffer, S.F. (1980) 'The unreality of realism', *Critical Inquiry* 6: 727–38.

Shoshan, T. (1989) 'Mourning and longing from generation to generation', *American Journal of Psychotherapy* 43(2): 193–207.

Sigal, J. (1971) 'Second generations effects of massive trauma', *International Psychiatry Clinics* 8: 55–65.

—— (1973) 'Hypotheses and methodology in the study of families of Holocaust survivors', in E.J. Anthony and C. Koupernik, ed.

The Child in His Family: The Impact of Disease and Death. New York: John Wiley, 2: 411–18.

Slipp, S. (1982) 'Introduction', in Samuel Slipp, ed. *Curative Effects in Dynamic Psychotherapy*, New York: McGraw-Hill.

Sonnenberg, S.M. (1974) 'Children of survivors: workshop report', *J. Amer. Psychoanal. Assn* 22: 200–04.

Spitz, R.A. (1956) 'Countertransference', *J. Amer. Psychoanal. Assn* 4: 256–65.

Szasz, T.S. (1957) 'A contribution to the psychology of bodily feelings', *Psychoanal. Q.* 26: 25–47.

Trossman, B. (1968) 'Adolescent children of concentration camp survivors', *Canadian Psychiatric Association Journal* 12: 122–3.

Wangh, M. (1968a) *Minutes of Discussion Group 6:* 'Children of social catastrophe'. Sequelae in survivors and the children of survivors. Meeting of American Pyschoanalytic Association, Boston, 1968.

—— (1968b) 'A psychogenetic factor in the recurrence of war: Symposium on psychic traumatisation through social catastrophe', *International Journal of Psychoanalysis* 49: 319–23.

Wardi, D. (1992) *Memorial Candles: Children of the Holocaust*. London: Routledge.

Wiesel, E. (1961) *The Accident*. New York: Bantam.

—— (1986) *The Fifth Son*. New York: Warner.

Wilson, A. (1985) 'On silence and the Holocaust. A contribution to clinical theory', *Psychoanalytic Inquiry* 5(1): 51–62.

Winnicott, D.W. (1958) 'The capacity to be alone', in *The Maturational Processes and the Facilitating Environment*. London: Hogarth, 1965.

—— (1962) 'Ego integration in child development,' in *The Maturational Processes and the Facilitating Environment*. London: Hogarth, 1965.

—— (1964) 'Correspondence: "Love or Skill?"', *New Society*, February.

—— (1965) *The Maturational Processes and the Facilitating Environment*. London: Hogarth.

—— (1971) 'The use of an object and relating through identification', in *Playing and Reality*. London: Tavistock.

Wisdom, J.O. (1970) 'Freud and Melanie Klein: psychology, ontology and weltanschaung', in C. Hanly and M. Lozerowitz eds, *Psychoanalysis and Philosophy*. New York: International University Press, pp. 327–62.

Zeligs, M. (1967) 'Acting in', *J. Amer. Psychoanal. Assn* 5: 685–706.

Index